POEM PRAYERS

Msgr. Charles D. McGlinn

PREFACE

$\mathcal{P}$oem Prayers began about 25 years ago as a conclusion to my homilies at Sunday Mass. It's good to have an ending. Otherwise I could just ramble on. So I tried to select three main points from the homily, and in verse, put them in the form of a prayer. As I was speaking the prayer, the organist would softly play some appropriate hymn in the background. (A little schmaltz is good for the soul).

Surprisingly, people seemed to like the prayers, and the teens were glad to hear the music heralding the end of the homily. After a while, some folks asked if I would publish the prayers. So I started putting together little booklets with a number of prayers which I then sent out to my parishioners.

At that time the parish had adopted an orphanage, Nuestros Pequeños Hermanos in Miacatlan, Mexico. It is a wonderful place, then administered by Fr. Phil Cleary, a truly great priest on loan from the Archdiocese of Chicago. This orphanage houses and cares for about 1,000 orphaned or abandoned children, who would otherwise try to survive on the streets and garbage dumps of the area.

This orphanage provides for the housing, food, clothing, education, medical services and all the love possible in this extended family. A unique feature setting this orphanage above other similar institutions is that no child is ever expelled. You don't fire your kids. And when this realization sets in, a profound change occurs in the life of these children. They finally belong somewhere where they are loved unconditionally. It makes all the difference.

So, I started sending out the Poem Prayers about a month before Christmas to all my parishioners, with a begging letter for the orphans. Happily there was a beautiful response, as there always has been with the wonderful people of Cure' of Ars Parish. Regardless of the literary quality of these poems, it's hard to say "no" to the orphans at Christmas.

This volume is a collection of many of the Poem Prayers I have used over the years. All the proceeds from the sale of this book, as well as any donations, will go to the benefit of these orphaned children in Mexico.

I hope that some of the offerings in this collection might inspire you and help to bring you closer to Jesus, as well as help our orphans in Mexico.

Msgr. Charles D. McGlinn recently retired as pastor of Cure' of Ars Parish located in Leawood, Kansas, after 28 years of priestly service there and a total of 48 years as a priest of the Archdiocese of Kansas City in Kansas.

ADORATION AND PRAISE

1.

Bridge To Life Eternal

O Jesus, Lord, you are the bridge
Spanning the waters deep,
Over danger, hardship and trial,
And many gorges steep.
Though many here will weep and wail,
Hell's gates shall not prevail.

This world of ours is not secure
For travelers to pass
In safety to the other side,
To God, to life. Alas.
Though we be blown in wind and gale
Hell's gates shall not prevail.

You are the bridge, in your being,
O God and man made one,
For us to go from here to God,
The victory has been won.
Though sin and death our lives assail,
Hells' gates shall not prevail.

Jesus Lord, you give us your Church,
Within, you do abide.
Your Church is now the bridge to life,
Across the threatening tide.
Though Satan works that we might fail,
Hell's gates shall not prevail.

2.

Christ The King

Jesus you are King of all
You come to judge the earth.
You judge unlike the ways of man
The last will be the first.

Compassion is your standard, Lord,
For the hungry and the least,
Humble service is your way
For our admittance to your feast.

We see you, Lord, with eyes of faith,
We long to see your face.
But when with love we help the poor
It is you whom we embrace.

King Jesus, Lord, Servant King,
Help us to follow you.
So that when you bring the end
Our life you will renew.

Poem Prayers

3.

Christ Our King

Jesus, Savior of the World,
Jesus Christ, our King,
You are Lord over all.
Our homage, today we bring.

Jesus, risen, glorified,
You reign upon a cross.
Suffering, loving, dying there,
Saving us through loss.

Your loss of life is our gain,
You are a Servant King.
You have nothing more to give.
You gave everything.

Your Kingdom, Lord, is within,
You rule o'er the heart.
Mind and heart and soul you claim,
From us never part.

Jesus, Savior, Christ our King,
Our foundation, center, core,
You are sovereign Lord, my God,
We worship and adore.

4.

Come, Spirit

Come, Spirit, Spirit come!
Impale me with your living flame.
Sanctify, unify
Our world, so full of strife and pain.

End our hate, hostility,
Fill our hearts with love Divine.
Our divisions, terminate,
Our souls and hearts now align.

Jesus, you came to make us one,
Your love for us is supreme.
You gave all for us, O Lord,
You came to save, and to redeem.

O touch our hearts, most precious Lord,
With your love uniting,
With holy longing to see your face,
Fill our inner being.

What is heaven yet to come?
What our destiny?
You want us all to share with you
Perfect peace and unity.

5.

Compassionate Jesus

Jesus, Lord of great compassion,
You know others' pain.
You feel the sorrow and the grief,
Their suff'ring you unchain.

You have the pow'r to heal the sick,
Your strength is from above.
You heal the body, mind and soul,
With your compass'nate love.

You have healed us too, O Lord,
Countless times before,
When we were hurt or greatly stressed,
Confused, in pain, heart-sore.

You call us as your instruments
To be your healers, too,
To reach out to all the world.
May all in us see you.

May we be compassionate, Lord,
To a world in great distress.
May we bring your healing, Lord,
To sooth, to love, to bless.

6.

Do You Love Me?

"Do you love me?" this you ask.
"Do you love me?" you want to know.
"Do you love me?" three times you query.
Yes, Lord Jesus, I love you so!

When you ask this, in my heart,
I see my sin and know such shame.
I denied you, O my Savior,
And my heart is filled with pain.

But your voice is filled with love,
Even though I failed the test,
You reach out to heal my life
With your gentle forgiveness.

You transform me with your words,
You send me forth as your own,
You call me to be your disciple,
To bring others to your throne.

Jesus, Yes, I do love you,
With your love my soul, come brand.
Be with me my whole life long,
I give to you all that I am.

7.

God of Passion

O God of Passion and desire,
You yearn and long for us.
You want us, to embrace and hold,
Your love is passionate.

You want our joy and happiness
You want our inner peace,
You pursue us, relentlessly,
Your desire will never cease.

Our lives are shabby, tattered, Lord.
Sin has marred our souls.
Our relationships have gone awry.
You want to make us whole.

Your passion for us is so great
To free us from all harm,
You became a human being
To enfold us in your arms.

Born a child in Bethlehem,
You did not think it loss.
You extend your arms so wide,
A preview of the cross.

Jesus, passionate, loving Lord,
You give yourself anew.
With outstretched arms, you wait for us.
Will we give ourselves to you?

8.

God Of Surprise

You take us by surprise, O God,
When we are off our guard.
You don't act like we expect,
Our ways you disregard.

Who could foresee your brilliant plan
To save humanity.
You sent your Son, the God-Made- Man
To restore our sanity.

To bring the world your peace and joy,
A virgin, maiden mild,
Conceived her babe and brought to us
The Savior, God's own child.

Who could know this little child,
So vulnerable and frail,
Contained the power and the might
To save us, without fail.

All you ask is faith and love,
To trust and hope in you,
To say "Yes" to do your will,
And care for others, too.

You do what we don't expect,
You open up our eyes.
You share your life; You dwell with us,
O God of great surprise.

9.

Holy Longing

Jesus, Lord, my God my all,
I long for you within.
My soul thirsts for you, my Lord,
Come, take away my sin.

You made me for yourself, O Lord,
To be one with you forever.
You call to me within my soul,
"Come, and leave me never."

Jesus, I long for other things,
That may harm my soul,
Power, pleasure, riches, fame,
These won't make me whole.

Only you can quench my thirst,
And fill up my desire.
Come to me and inflame me,
With your holy fire.

Enlighten me, and be to me
Morning sun now dawning,
Fill my heart and fill my soul,
Fill my holy longing.

10.

Holy Trinity

O Father God, You have spoken
From all eternity,
To us your children here on earth,
With generosity.

O Word made Flesh, You dwell with us,
You are the Father's Word.
We who see you, see also Him,
Believing what we've heard.

Holy Spirit, divinely sent
To help us understand.
Teach us all truth that Jesus taught
And what he now commands.

Trinity, three persons divine,
One Divinity,
You love us and you dwell within,
O Holy Trinity.

Renew us with your love and light,
Hold us close to you,
That we might find salvation, Lord,
With love, our lives embue.

11.

I Belong to You

Jesus, I belong to you,
I am yours forevermore.
Your possession, your domain.
You are Lord whom I adore.

Take my life and change, dear Lord,
My inner spirit with your touch.
I repent of all my sins
Which offend you, Lord, so much.

Change the garments that I wear
Which keep me from you, apart,
My selfish words, deeds and thoughts,
Please, Lord, change my heart.

Help me give up my former ways,
My selfish negativity.
Help me walk throughout my life.
With justice, love, humility.

I am yours, O Lord, my God,
That is my joy, my hope, my pride.
Though I am poor, I am yours,
Savior, Lord, with me abide.

12.
I Long For You

There is a holy longing
Within my very soul,
A thirst and a hungering
An empty, aching hole.

I feel it when alone
With time to meditate
Or when life seems to drone
And fails to captivate.

Pleasure, fame, and power
And money, I have enough,
I need to grow, to flow'r,
To see, to hear, to touch.

It's you, my God, my Lord,
Whom I so now desire
I want my heart to soar,
My soul to be on fire.

I get glimpses, now and then,
Like shadows on a wall,
Like lead rods you can bend,
Apt to fail and fall.

Come to me, Lord, now,
Come, do not delay,
I love you, Lord, allow
Me with you to stay.

To stay in your embrace,
Fulfilled in you, O Lord,
Come to me, make haste,
Fill me to my core.

13.

Indwelling Lord

Jesus, Lord, you have revealed
That within you dwell,
With the Father, Spirit, too,
There, our fears you quell.

Loving Father, Incarnate Love
Loving Spirit, too,
Your dwelling place here on earth
Our hearts, you now renew.

Help us express your presence, Lord,
In all we say and do.
May your love be always found
Within us, reflecting you.

O Jesus Lord, make us like you
Fill us with your grace,
Enable all we meet, dear Lord,
To see in us your face.

14.

Jesus, Our Unity

O Lord, we are divided,
Walls and barriers we have made,
Fear and hate consume us,
From you we have all strayed.

Once long ago you came to earth.
You came to unify,
You came with mercy and with love,
You came to sanctify.

You have created within each heart
A longing and desire
To be one with you and all mankind
To love with holy fire.

Send your Spirit upon us, Lord,
Come to us once more,
Heal our sad divisions, Lord,
Your peace on us outpour.

Fill us with true Christmas joy,
With love and hope and peace
Unify and sanctify,
May our conflicts cease.

15.

Jesus The Vine

Jesus, Lord, you are the Vine,
Bearing fruit throughout time,
Giving glory, honor too,
To the Father, who loves you,
Loving him in all you do.

True Vine of Yaweh bearing fruit,
Fruitful vine on faithful root.
But the greatest mystery:
You joined us in unity,
To You, the vine, so graciously.

So great is shown your love for us,
How wonderful and glorious,
You are closer than we know,
On us your favor you bestow,
In us your graces overflow.

As branches, we are joined to you:
In us your very life runs through.
This mystery you institute
So that we might bear much fruit.
For the Father, bear much fruit.

16.

Jesus, Our King

Jesus, you fulfill the plan
Formed so long ago
When God created humankind.
What love to us you show.

Adam and Eve God made with love,
In his very own likeness.
He wanted them to thrive and grow
In joy and peace, endless.

But they soon disobeyed God's will,
And they fell from grace.
You promised us a Savior, Lord,
To save the human race.

King David then you sent to us
To rule and govern well
But he sinned too; he failed the test.
Our hopes for mankind fell.

Then one day the Angel came
And Mary he addressed
Would she consent to have a Son.
And Mary then said "Yes".

Jesus, Savior, joined to us,
Wondrous hope you bring.
You gave your life, and rose again.
You are Christ, our King.

17.

Jesus

Jesus, Lord, one with us,
We are the Body of Christ,
Born from above in your love,
You give us eternal life.

We are your church, O Jesus Lord,
Living in love and faith,
Joined to you and each other,
With you we're home, and safe.

You call us all to follow you,
To give, to love and serve,
You are our model and our joy,
Your grace we don't deserve.

You are here, with us you dwell,
You give us happiness,
You give us hope,and meaning too,
you promise life in fullness.

Thank you, Lord for your gift,
The gift like none other,
The gift of life, of love and joy,
The gift of one another.

18.

King Jesus

Jesus, King of heaven and earth,
Bring your kingdom now to birth.
Rule o'er all our hearts and lives,
May your peace on earth arrive,
And your praises reach the skies.

Jesus, your love is so great,
A love we're called to imitate.
You are always with us, Lord,
On us your blessings are outpoured,
Our lives to be for you reformed.

Lord Jesus, our hearts now inspire,
With love for you, set us afire,
Draw us to you, God's only Son,
Our salvation you have won,
Hungry, thirsty, now we come.

We want to build your kingdom here,
With justice, peace, an end to fear,
With inner joy, tranquility,
Creating true serenity,
Respecting each one's dignity.

Lord, we fall on bended knee,
May we your people ever be,
King of Kings and Lord of Lords,
Before you, Jesus, we adore,
You will rule forevermore.

19.

Living Water

Jesus, Lord, come quench my thirst.
Help me turn to you.
In my heart become the first
To love in all I do.

Without you, Lord, I am so dry,
I thirst with parched lips.
Nothing seems to satisfy.
Have you water I might sip?

Renew me at your fountain deep,
Renew, O Lord, my heart.
Close to you, Lord, my life keep,
From you ne'er to part.

Your presence quenches all my thirst,
Your words well up in me.
In your love I am immersed,
Within me, ever be.

20.

Lord of All

You are Lord of all the earth
You are Lord of everything.
The universe you have made
You are our Ground of Being.

We pray to you, O Lord above,
And Lord within my heart
Help us in our neediness
Never from us part.

Without you, Lord, there is no hope
No meaning, no reason for
Working, striving, living on,
It's hopeless, forevermore.

But with you, Lord, there is joy,
Blessed peace is ours.
With your presence and your grace,
The seeds of life will flower.

Come to us and change our hearts,
Come, our lives transform,
Transform our world, so full of fear,
Come, dear Lord, please come.

21.

Lord of Eternity

Jesus, Lord of earth and sky,
We belong to you.
We know not when the end will come,
But we trust in you.

If we live a long, long life,
Life is still so brief.
Eternity beckons all,
The end comes like a thief.

Jesus, Lord, help us prepare
To see and welcome you
By living life with living faith
And love in all we do.

We trust your love; we trust in you.
Your love will never cease.
Hold us gently in your arms,
Grant us perfect peace.

22.

Lord of Joy

Jesus, Lord, come walk with me.
I believe and trust in Thee.
I know well your love is great,
Come, and all my fears abate.

Your love for us is without end,
All our hurts your care will mend.
Your love for us is so profound,
We can't express the joy we've found.

Joy in being loved by you,
Joy in loving others, too.
To walk with you throughout life,
Changes sorrow, transforms strife.

You touch our hearts and inner self,
You feed our hunger with yourself.
You call us to feed others, too,
To bring your love in all we do.

Jesus, Lord, come walk with me.
Your light and truth now let me see.
My fear and hatred, come destroy,
Come, dear Jesus, Lord of Joy.

23.

Lord of Justice

You came to heal our world, O Lord,
You are Lord, most just,
Your own mission you give your church,
Your justice, you entrust.

Our Father made each human being
In his very likeness.
We can know and we are free;
No one is valueless.

Our dignity is greater still
Because you came to earth.
You made us God's own family,
You gave us second birth.

Every person, because of this
Has rights and dignity.
In justice, we must each respect,
And treat each fittingly.

Help us, Lord, to be like you,
Your justice to reflect,
In our words and in our deeds,
Our neighbor to respect.

24.

Lord of Life

O God of love, O Lord of life,
What have I ever done
To deserve your choice that I should live,
To grow, to laugh, to run?

From all eternity, O Lord,
You knew me, loved me too.
You called me forth from nothingness,
You watched me as I grew.

You formed me, Lord, within the womb,
My mother felt me there
As I moved, and kicked, and cried,
Her life, and yours, I share.

I thank you, Lord, for my life,
For bringing me to earth.
I thank you for my family,
I thank you for my birth.

We have many choices, Lord,
Which bring us joy or strife,
We rule over many things,
But you are Lord of Life.

25.

Lord of Peace

Jesus, come and bring your peace,
All my fear control.
I feel alone and on my own,
With peace, come fill my soul.

Send your Spirit, infuse my life,
Send him to teach and guide,
Show me that I'm not alone,
Within me, you abide.

You and the Father dwell within,
My very life, your home.
I put my life into your hands,
O Lord, I am your own.

I surrender to your will,
What you want I must
Give completely, humbly too,
With total faith and trust.

Jesus, come and calm my fears,
Your presence never cease.
Soothe my worry and dismay,
Come, Jesus, Lord of Peace.

26.

Lord of Strength

Jesus, you are my strength and hope
When things are going wrong.
When bad things occur in life,
It is you who makes me strong.

Give me patience, give me strength,
Help me endure the tide
Of conflict, fear and violence,
Stay, Lord, by my side.

Lord, I place into your hands
All my pain and fear.
I trust in you; I can go on,
Knowing you are near.

Be with me today, my Lord,
A mountain I must cross.
Lift up my heart; show me the way,
So I won't get lost.

27.

Lord of the Sabbath

Lord of the Sabbath, be Lord of my heart.
Rule over my life, never to part.
Fill me with faith, with hope and with love,
Fill me with grace from heaven above.

Lord of the Sabbath, before you I come,
Filled with thanksgiving for all you have done.
I bow down before you, telling my need
Of your loving presence. My life you must lead.

Lead me and guide me along the right road.
Give me your strength to carry my load.
In my heart and soul, you I enthrone,
I adore you my Jesus, I am your own.

Lord of the Sabbath, Lord of my life,
Give me your peace in a world filled with strife,
You are my Savior, You are my Lord.
Lord of the Sabbath, I bow down and adore.

28.

May We Be One

Jesus, Lord, you prayed for us
When your life on earth was done.
Summing up your mission, Lord,
You prayed that we be one.

One in love and one in peace,
Our unity you desire,
One in you, with you in us,
Inflame us with your fire.

Jesus, Lord, dwelling within,
In you peace and justice meet.
You send us all into the world
Your mission to complete.

We are reconcilers, Lord,
Our work is to unify.
Our world torn in violence
You call us to pacify.

Dwell within us, saving Lord,
Unite our lives with you.
Send your Spirit so we may
Create our world anew.

29.

New Adam, New Creation

Beloved Son of God divine,
Sent to form a new mankind,
Our new Adam, the first born son,
Our salvation you have won.
To you our lives unite and bind.

By the Godhead you were fathered,
Over you the Spirit hovered,
Making you the new foundation
For his work of re-creation
Of the world, it's people gathered.

Gathered to be one with you,
United with each other, too,
In harmony and unity,
With justice, peace, solidarity,
One with you in all we do.

Jesus, Lord, be with us now,
Before you, Lord, we kneel and bow
Our heads and hearts in adoration,
We give to you total dedication.
With love and joy our lives endow.

30.

Pond Wisps

Have you ever looked and seen
Pond water, early morn,
Sun cracking midnight dark,
Mourning doves, forlorn.

Stillness, and yet, I see,
The mist rising, faithfully,
Translucent, like windows,
Cathedralesque, holy.

Fragile, and dispersing,
Rising cloudy mist,
Wisps like smoke, from heated heart,
Blown, patchy, wisps,

Like the prayers of my heart
Rising with the sun,
Dissipating, though heaven sent,
And now, heaven won.

31.

Thank you, Lord

Lord, I wish to give you thanks,
You bless abundantly.
You are always there for me,
Though I don't always see.

You are the source of life itself,
You gave me faith and family.
I have a home, I have my health,
And my eternal destiny.

Teach me to put my trust in you,
You who're always there,
You've blessed my past, you bless me now,
I'm always in your care.

You gave all you had for me,
You died upon that cross,
You found me and brought me back,
When I was truly lost.

With all my family here today
All with one accord
We lift our hearts and souls to pray,
And say, "Thank you, Lord."

32.

The Baptism of Jesus

John's Baptism was for sin,
The many sins of all
"Repent", and, "Turn to God",
This was the Baptist's call.

Why, then Jesus, did you go
Into the Jordan too?
You, the sinless Son of God,
What is this you do?

Was it to show that you are one
With all who are in need
Of God's love and kind mercy,
That these you want to lead?

Then lead me, Lord, with all the rest;
Sinners we are all.
Help us repent, forgive us now,
Help us hear your call.

Help us too be one with you,
And one with all the poor,
One with the lost and suffering,
With those who need you more.

33.

The Lamb Of God

Jesus, loving innocent Lamb,
You are the Lamb of God.
You came to earth because of love,
And on our path you trod.

Jesus, Lord, O Lamb of God,
O Lamb of sacrifice,
For our sins, upon the cross,
You paid the awful price.

Triumphant, risen Lamb of God,
O Lamb upon the throne,
All praise and glory now are yours,
And heaven is your home.

Lamb of God, make us loving, too,
And take away our sins.
Share with us your glory, Lord,
Our hearts, abide within.

34.

Transfigured Jesus

Jesus, Lord, you dwell within,
In my heart and life.
You give me strength, you give me hope,
In the midst of strife.

You speak to me within my heart,
Direction you kindly give.
In my conscience, in my soul
You tell me how to live.

Transfigured Jesus, Transfigure me,
Change my life today.
Help me listen to your voice,
This, I humbly pray.

Let your light within me shine,
Cast out all my sin,
You who dwell within my heart,
You who dwell within.

35.

Transfigured

Jesus, at that darkest time
When you faced your death,
When you faced the suffering
That would be your guest,

As you recoiled from violence,
The cross that men would hew,
You prayed to God your Father
Who could deliver you.

Instead of pain preventing,
And suffering decrease,
He showed you the glory
That would never cease.

"If you have faith and courage
You have the victory won.
Know that I am with you,
You are my beloved son"

Jesus, now be with us,
As we face life's pain,
Help us listen closely,
He tells us the same.

36.

Trinity

God, our God, O blessed be!
Revealed to us as Trinity.
Three, yet one, O God on high,
We, your name, now glorify.

Father, God of power and might,
Creator of the dark and light,
In awe we worship and we sing.
In you we live and have our being.

Jesus, Son, the Word made Flesh,
With us now, you are our guest.
You redeem and save, O Lord,
We sing your praise with one accord.

Spirit, Mover, sanctify!
Fill our hearts with love, we cry.
Fill our universe with peace,
Never let your mercy cease.

O Trinity, O Unity,
You are one and yet are three.
We bow down and we adore,
We are yours forevermore.

37.

Unless

Unless you build, we build in vain.
Unless you bring the sun and rain,
Unless you make the seed to grow,
We have no life; we have no hope.

Unless you touch our sinful hearts
With the grace you can impart,
Unless you touch, forgive and heal,
Whole, we will not be, nor feel.

Unless you knock upon our door,
Unless you mend what is torn,
Unless you open up the skies,
Useless are our feeble cries.

Unless you stay with us today,
Unless you show us the way,
Unless you give your love and light,
We are lost in darkest night.

Jesus, Lord, you are our hope;
Place on us your easy yoke.
Fill us with your power and might,
Against all evil, help us fight.

38.

Who Are You, Jesus?

Who are you, Jesus? How can I know?
I want to see you. Where Can I go?
Where can I go to see and to know?

"Come in my name, come two or three,
Come with your faith, come and now see.
Come in your love, come, with me be."

"Hear now my Word, hear and believe.
Hear now my voice, your fears I relieve.
Listen to me. In my Gospel, perceive."

"Now in this Bread, now in this Cup,
Meet me and know me. Fill yourself up
With my Flesh and my Blood. Fill yourself up."

Come to me now in the needy and poor,
With your compassion, touch the heart-sore.
You do unto me, when love you outpour."

"When you are tired and hurting, you'll see,
When you are burdened, come unto me.
I will refresh you. Come, with me be."

39.

Who Are You?

"Who are you, Jesus? Are you the One?
Were you sent by God? Are you his Son?"
To these words of John Baptist, you did reply,
"Look at my actions. They do not lie."

"My work is to heal, to pardon, to free
All the imprisoned, all who can't see.
I come with compassion, with love and with peace,
God's love and forgiveness will never cease."

Thank you, my Jesus, for coming to me.
Thank you, Lord Jesus, for helping me see.
I want to be like you, your image on earth,
To serve and to love, bringing kindness to birth.

Help me to change, and become more like you,
Not only in words, but in what I do.
Help me to grow, like seed you have sown.
I am your possession. I am your own.

40.

Who is Jesus?

Jesus, you are Savior, Lord,
Son of God, revered, adored.
You are life itself, to me,
From my sins, you set me free.
You, creation's apogee.

Jesus, you are Teacher, too,
Giving purpose to life that's true,
O dear Jesus, teach me your way,
Be my model, for every day,
Your call to me, I will obey.

Jesus, Lord, you are my friend,
Into my life the Father sent
To strengthen, comfort, and to heal,
Your loving presence, help me feel,
Give me the peace and joy that is real.

Jesus, Lord, Teacher, and Friend,
You offer us, life without end.
Be with us now, Lord, we implore,
Oneness with you, we ask you, restore,
We thank you, Jesus, whom we adore.

41.

With Eyes Fixed On Jesus

Help us keep our eyes on you,
Fixed unflinchingly.
Jesus, Lord, you are the Lord,
Strength for our fragility,
Source of our stability.

When life's conflicts overwhelm,
When we feel the pain,
Help us then to understand
With us you remain,
In sunshine, and in rain.

In time of doubt or weakness, Lord,
When tempted to pursue
What is evil, sinful, wrong,
Show us what is true.
Keep our eyes fixed on you.

When I divert my gaze from you,
And seek some lesser goal,
Risking all for worthless things,
Riding for a fall,
Give me wisdom, self-control.

Give me courage to speak out
When injustice threatens to
Hurt and harm your purpose, Lord,
Show me what to do.
Keep my eyes fixed on you.

42.

Word Made Flesh

O God, you love us each so much
With love, unending too.
You want to dwell with us fore'er,
Bringing life to us anew.

You are so far beyond us, Lord,
Transcendent, mysterious,
And so, that we would love you, too,
You were born a babe, like us.

You whom the world could not contain,
Are born a babe, so mild.
In heaven you did not remain.
You became a human child.

Jesus, my God, King of Kings,
Savior, Redeemer, Lord,
To your greatness you did not cling,
Human clothes you wore.

The shepherds came, full of awe.
The angels sang to them.
They found you in a cave on straw,
Newborn King of Bethlehem.

Will we love you, you want to know,
Will we believe and see?
To Bethlehem will our hearts go?
Adoring on bended knee?

DISCIPLESHIP

43.

A Disciple's Prayer

Jesus, I want to follow you,
And your disciple be.
Be in the first place in my life.
Give me fidelity.

Sometimes I'm tempted to look back,
The way things were before
You came into my heart and life,
And made my spirit soar.

I'm distracted by many things,
By fame and fortune too,
Money, power, these attract me;
Pleasure can faith undo.

I do not want to compromise
My promises to you.
You are my Lord, my only God,
Please help me to be true.

I am your disciple, Lord,
I am also weak.
Strengthen your poor servant, Lord.
To serve you, this I seek.

44.

Be Perfect

"Be Perfect", Lord, is your command,
But I don't really understand.
It's hard for me to take it in,
When my life is so full of sin.

"Turn the other cheek" you say
Forgive today, without delay.
Take another with a smile.
When you're forced to go one mile.

Give your shirt, as well your coat,
To serve, to give, your life devote.
"I am here, to see you through,
My grace, my love, I give anew."

You are the only perfect one,
Perfection, no, I have none,
Only the gift of your sweet love,
Given freely from above.

Your life you want to share with me,
Your very own divinity,
"Be perfect" means be one with you,
Forever, for all eternity.

45.

At The Well

Jesus at the well that day
You came to quench a thirst
You offered life to the Samar'tan,
You made the least the first.

You gave that woman dignity
Belief in you she gave,
Living waters you poured out
Water to heal and save.

Touch my heart again, O Lord,
Change my life once more,
Pour out your Spirit on me, Lord,
Transform me at the core.

You are the Way, the Truth, the Life,
Teach with wisdom true,
How to live life to the fullest,
In following after you.

Quench my thirst, O Savior Lord,
With waters ever new,
The Water of your Spirit, Lord,
My thirst is thirst for you.

46.

Be With Me Today

Jesus, help me see you today
As you come to show the way
To live in faith and charity,
Please, give me eyes to see.

Be with me in family,
Help me love you tenderly
In those so special, in my home,
Those who are my very own.

You are here in all my friends,
On their friendship I depend.
Wherever there is peace and joy,
Your gentle presence I enjoy.

Jesus, Lord of all the poor
And suffering, you I adore.
I want to serve you in your need,
To comfort, clothe, to share, to feed.

Jesus, be with me today,
Come into my life to stay.
Loving Lord, abide with me;
You are here. Help me see.

47.

Be With Us

Jesus, you have come.
Jesus, you are here.
Jesus, you will come again,
Soon you will appear.

What joy you bring to us, O Christ,
Even in our pain,
Our losses and our sorrows, too,
In you, our loss is gain.

You were born a human being,
Though Son of God you are.
You are always close at hand,
Close and never far.

You are also coming, Lord,
When death we will all taste.
Then we will be one with you,
We'll see you face to face.

Be with us now, Emmanuel,
Our tears and fears destroy.
Be with us always, O my God,
Bring us your peace and joy.

48.

Beatitude

You show the way to blessedness,
And happiness as well,
It's found in making of our hearts
A place where you can dwell.

Poor in spirit, those who mourn,
The meek and humble, too,
They make room within their lives,
For relationship with you.

Hungering not for power or fame,
But for what is right,
To be merciful, and clean of heart
Is true strength and might.

Blessed are the peacemakers,
If it may seem odd
In a world of hateful violence,
You are a child of God.

In suffering persecution
Pain, rejection, loss,
For the cause of Jesus Christ,
We then share his cross.

True holiness and happiness
Can be yours, I say,
By hearing and by living now
The Beatitudes today.

49.

Black and White

Life is not just black or white,
There are shades of grey.
Mixed in life are good and bad,
Help me see, I pray.

When I judge by what I see
Only externally,
I mistake the good and bad,
Erring miserably.

It's within, O Lord, you know,
Truth is in the heart.
Give me insight, help me see,
Wisdom, please, impart.

Or help me not to judge at all
My neighbor to condemn.
Only actions, they're the fruits,
By their fruits you shall know them.

50.

Be Perfect

"Be Perfect", Lord, is your command,
But I don't really understand.
It's hard for me to take it in,
When my life is so full of sin.

"Turn the other cheek" you say
Forgive today, without delay.
Take another with a smile.
When you're forced to go one mile.

Give your shirt, as well your coat,
To serve, to give, your life devote.
"I am here, to see you through,
My grace, my love, I give anew."

You are the only perfect one,
Perfection, no, I have none,
Only the gift of your sweet love,
Given freely from above.

Your life you want to share with me,
Your very own divinity,
"Be perfect" means be one with you,
Forever, for all eternity.

51.

At The Door

Jesus Knocking at my door,
You come to me, the least of all,
You search out the sick and poor,
You find the lost and prodigal.

You don't force your will, your way,
O power of the universe.
You invite those gone astray;
You entice, and not coerce.

Jesus, you are standing there
Hoping I will hear your call.
How often I am unaware,
Oblivious, and forgetful.

I want to open up the door
Of my heart and life to you.
Be with me forevermore.
Forgive my sins, my life renew.

Jesus, enter, dine with me.
Share with me your life, my Lord.
I am blind, please help me see,
Jesus, knocking at my door.

52.

God's Love

Jesus, you were sent by God
The Father, our Creator,
You came to earth for our rebirth,
You are Lord and Savior.

Such love the Father has for us
He did not spare his Son,
You suffered much and died at last,
So that we'd be one.

One with you, his only Son,
For all eternity.
One as his children, his very own,
You confer nobility.

You came to earth so long ago
Born in a humble cave,
You came, beloved Son of God,
Not to condemn, but save.

For God so loved this world of ours,
In spite of sinfulness,
You were crucified for us
To show God's graciousness.

53.

Call to Greatness

Jesus, lord, you are the way,
You show us how to live.
The path to greatness is to love,
To serve and generously give.

To sacrifice for your Church
Out of love for you, O Christ,
That's the way to be truly great,
And also truly wise.

Help us, Lord, to listen to
Your call to join with you.
You are the way, the truth, the life.
You show us what to do.

You are the suffering servant, Lord,
You gave all, on a cross of wood.
For us you died. With us abide.
Let us share your servanthood.

Servant Jesus, for us all
You opened heaven's gate,
And showed the way to live each day
And to be truly great.

54.

Cast Again

"Cast your net into the deep,
Trust me, Cast your net."
I hear your call within my heart,
Your voice I can't forget.

Lord, I've done this through the night,
All to no avail.
But, I will do as you ask,
Knowing I will fail.

"Trust in me and trust my word,
Trust my love and call.
Cast out again into the deep,
Fear not to give your all."

Thank you, Lord. How could I doubt,
How could I fail to see
That when I trust in you and act
You are there with me?

With me, Lord, to overcome
All fear of pain and strife.
When I cast into the deep,
Lord, you change my life.

55.

Come After Me

"Come after me", Jesus you say,
"Be fishers of men", you call us today.
"Be my disciples, come close to me,
I will teach you and guide you,
And set your hearts free."

O Jesus, dear Master, we hear your call.
Let our "yes" be, unconditional.
You want us to come now, without delay,
You want us to follow
With you always to stay.

You call us, dear Jesus, to spend time with you,
To develop within a love that is true.
To be your disciples, to be your dear friends,
To love you and serve you,
To love without end.

You send us forth to bring your Good News
To all who are hungry, thirsty, abused.
To help the downtrodden, to help the blind see,
Witnessing to your Gospel of life,
To answer your call, "Come after me."

56.

Come To Me

"Come to me," are words you say,
Your arms are open wide.
You call to me to come to you,
A scar still marks your side.

O Jesus, Lord, to you I come.
To come to you, I must.
Into your hands, I place my life,
With faith and love and trust.

"Learn from me," are words I hear,
Words to free my life
From sin and death and emptiness,
From needless pain and strife.

Gentle Jesus with humble heart,
Help me follow you.
Change all angry arrogance
To love in all I do.

Yoked to you, a yoke you made,
To help me on life's road,
With you near me, side by side,
We'll pull any load.

57.

Diamonds In The Rough

Jesus Lord, you know us all
We have faults and sins enough.
But you see, possibility;
We're diamonds in the rough.

You loves us all. You give us all.
You know we're not so tough,
We need your care and polishing,
We're diamonds in the rough.

Help us see, as you do see,
Beyond the outward stuff,
To the heart, the inner soul,
To the diamond in the rough.

When I'm tempted to insult,
Demean or hurl rebuff,
Help me see your love for me,
And the diamond in the rough.

58.

Friend of the Poor

Jesus, friend of all the poor,
Your blessings you announce
On those who trust in only you,
And trust in wealth, renounce.

"Blessed Poor" and "Woeful Rich"
Refer not to how much gold
Or possessions that we own,
But the trust that our hearts hold.

Trust in God, the source of all,
Life itself, our talents too,
You teach us trust, and that real
Security is found in you.

Whether rich or whether poor,
You love all infinitely.
You want us to share and to care,
To help, with generosity.

Jesus, friend of all the poor,
Help us good stewards be,
Building your Kingdom here on earth,
With the poor, in solidarity.

59.

God's Face

"Show us the Father. That's enough,"
Phillip said once to you.
"O show us now the face of God,
Living, and ever true."

But, Lord, you are the Son of God,
Joined to the human race.
In looking at your marvelous life,
We now behold God's face.

O Christ, you are God's only Word,
How he expressed himself.
The Godhead, you reveal to us
And share with us true wealth.

The wealth that comes from following you,
You are the only Way,
The riches shared abundantly
In following every day.

O, you are the Truth, shining bright,
The Truth for all to see,
Yes, near and clear and ever dear,
The Truth to set us free.

You are the Life, eternal Life,
Life lived abundantly.
You share your life; you gave your life,
To raise the dead like me.

You are my Way, my Truth, my Life,
Be ever at my side.
Show and teach , revive me, my Lord,
And be my saving guide.

60.

Good Samaritan Prayer

Lord, help us feel the needs of others
To taste the pain unknown,
Except by sisters and by brothers.
Compassion makes their needs our own.

There are limits, Lord, and barriers
Between your family,
Preventing kindness, generous care,
Loving, unconditionally.

Culture, race, get in the way,
Religion sometimes, too,
Of creating a whole new day,
Where love's the heart of all we do.

Make us like the Good Samar'tan
Fill our hearts with generosity,
Compassion, kindness, to be certain,
With you, we'll spend eternity.

61.

Help me say "Yes"

To your desires, I want to say "yes",
To all that you want of me.
When I say "no", I offend you so,
And prevent the good that could be.

When I seek first my own will,
Selfishness comes through,
It's my own pleasure that I seek,
Instead of serving you.

Empty heart and empty life,
This I'm destined for,
Unless I learn to love you, Lord,
And seek to serve you more.

Jesus, you are my guide through life,
I want to be the best.
Give me strength to follow you,
Help me to say "Yes".

62.

Humble Jesus

Humble Jesus, teach us, Lord,
To take the lowest place,
To live our lives in service here,
Strengthened by your grace.

Take away all arrogance,
Purify our hearts.
Pattern our lives after yours,
Humility impart.

Give us joy in serving you.
With compassion, gift our lives,
For your poor and suffering.
In us charity revive.

You are our example, Lord,
Of true humility.
Gentle servant of us all,
You tell us, "Learn from me."

If we take the lowest place,
Humble service, our desire,
When our life is over here,
You'll tell us, "Come up higher."

63.

I Don't Get It

Sometimes, Lord, I can not see.
Your purpose often escapes me.
Why am I here? Where will I go?
Your plans for me I do not know.
I don't get it.

Sometimes the pain of life is great.
Why does suffering permeate
The whole world? If we are your own,
Why do I feel so alone?
I don't get it.

Sometimes, Lord, I hear you knock,
But my door, I often lock
For fear of what might hurt me,
Or fear of what I cannot see.
I don't get it.

You came to earth so long ago,
Your perfect love still overflows,
You gave all upon a tree,
On a cross you set me free,
You gave your life for love of me.
Lord, now I get it.

64.

Jesus, Interrupted

Jesus Lord, you show the way
To live life graciously,
With mercy, love and pity too.
You lived unselfishly

When it was convenient to,
Indeed you did respond.
But also when it wasn't so,
Your love was deep and strong.

When you were interrupted, Lord,
You were not upset,
When you were imposed upon,
You did not fume or fret.

Jesus, interrupted,
Inconvenienced by the crowd,
You card and shared and ministered,
With great love you are endowed.

65.

Just Passing Through

Lord, I get caught up in material things,
I want things old and new,
I have so many worldly thoughts,
But I know I'm passing through.
I'm just passing through.

Why do things obsess me, Lord,
When my greatest need is You?
Material matters make me forget,
That I'm just passing through.
I'm just passing through.

A lot of stuff clutters up my life,
My heart and mind renew,
Remind me, Lord, Help me to see
That I'm just passing through.
I'm just passing through.

It's my relationships that matter most
With others and with you.
Love is the most important thing,
Cause I'm just passing through;
I'm just passing through.

66.

Justice and Mercy Meet

O Jesus Lord, most merciful
Source of blessedness,
In your infinite love for us
Mercy's one with justice.

You gave all to forgive our sins,
On Calvary's cruel cross,
Our guilt was taken all away,
Mercy restored our loss.

But you call us to change our hearts,
Grace lends the ability.
Because you love us, you require
Our accountability.

Accountability for our lives,
For a life complete,
In your wisdom and your love,
Justice and mercy meet.

Loving Jesus be with me,
Through all joy and strife
Help me to live aright,
All throughout my life.

67.

Lazarus

Lazarus was here, full of sores,
Hungry, a casualty.
I didn't harass or hate him.
Him, I did not see.

He was poor, like so many more,
What was I to do?
It's the way it is, after all.
They'll always be with you.

Why was he poor and destitute?
The shape that he was in?
Was it his fault, was it his fate?
Was it caused by his sins?

Don't look at me. I didn't see.
I did not cause his grief.
Why blame me? I didn't know.
He might have been a thief.

Lazarus is here, with us still.
See him in the other,
The one who's different from you,
Lazarus is your brother.

68.

Let Go

Jesus Lord, I can't let go.
Although I hear your call.
I want to follow after you
but I can't give up all,

All my money, all I own.
Is that what you really want?
Then why did you first bless me so?
Was it to tease and taunt?

I know you have a plan for me,
Greatness might be mine.
You tell me first I must let go,
And trust your grand design.

To love you first, and things last,
All things material,
Seek first the things that really last,
That which is spiritual.

"Don't hang on or be attached,"
You want me to know,
"Be free, be filled with God's mercy,
Open your hands, let go."

69.

Loaves and Fishes

The crowds of hungry people, Lord,
Are so great and vast.
How can we give them bread to eat,
The hungry and outcast.

"You give them to eat, yourselves,"
Are words that you once said,
You say again to us today
As you give us Living Bread.

"Put your gifts into my hands,"
This is your command.
Our meager gifts you multiply,
If each gives as each can.

Nourish us, O Jesus whom
In this Eucharist we meet.
And help us answer your request:
"Give them something yourselves to eat."

70.

My Pledge

Lord, I offer you my life;
All I say and do
Is dedicated to your will,
I pledge myself to you.

When I'm tempted to leave you,
To disregard your call,
Remind me Lord, and strengthen me
To give to you my all.

When I wander away from you,
Perhaps in pain or strife,
Lord, where could I ever go,
You have the words of life.

Jesus, you gave all for me
With love that does not quit.
I want to always be with you,
To you, my life commit.

71.

My Prayer For Peace

Bring peace to our world, Lord Jesus,
Your blessed peace, please bring,
Please end this war between peoples,
Our hearts are hardening.

Our family apart is breaking,
Fighting with each other,
In the shedding of blood we hurt
Only ourselves and our brothers.

In this war everyone loses,
In this war we all dearly pay,
Sons and daughters dying,
Children in tombs we lay.

We are your family together,
From hate and fear release
Our hearts and those of our neighbors,
Bring us abiding peace.

Jesus, my dear Lord in heaven,
Love among us increase,
Fill us with faith and hope,
Bring us your blessed peace.

72.

No Other Hands

Jesus works through you and me.
As once the multitude he fed,
He feeds others through our care,
Through us he multiplies the bread.

Jesus needs your hands and mine.
As once he healed the lame,
He touches wounds again today
When we touch others' pain.

Jesus' truth and light still shine
In your truth and your strong word.
Others hear through you his truth,
As from his mouth once others heard.

So give yourself to Jesus' work.
Without your love the world grows worse.
Feed and heal and teach for him.
He has no other hands but yours.

73.

Prayer For Perseverance

Jesus, help us persevere
Through all our pain and trials,
Give us courage, give us faith,
Stay with us awhile.

When we face dangerous times,
Violence, hatred, fraud,
Through our faith and bravery,
Show the hand of God.

Help us keep on going, Lord,
Witnessing our faith,
By trusting, hoping, helping
Others' fears abate.

When we get discouraged, Lord,
When we are afraid,
Strengthen us with your strength,
Send your mighty aid.

When darkness nears and evil looms
Threatening to maraud
Be within our fearful hearts,
Show the hand of God.

74.

Prayer of the Steward

Jesus, you are Lord of all,
My life belongs to you,
All I am and all I have,
My time and talents, too.

Through you, Lord, I came to be,
By you I have been blessed.
You ask me now to follow you,
To serve, and to say "Yes."

Let me your disciple be,
A good steward of my gifts.
To give back to you, O Lord,
A heart of love I lift.

Jesus, you gave all for me,
Suffering and death endured.
This was your sweet offering,
Our heaven you ensured.

Use our gifts for your Kingdom, Lord,
Use them for the poor,
Let them serve your church on earth,
In this, they're heaven's door.

75.

Presentation Prayer

When your parents presented you,
Fulfilling ancient law,
They dedicated you to serve,
Reversing our downfall.

Your parents gave themselves to God
Offering to him
All they were and would become,
All God willed of them.

Now they offer you, dear Lord,
And you will do the same
Later on Calvary's cross,
To take away our shame.

Take my heart and soul as well,
I offer you my all
I dedicate my life to you
I have heard your call.

Jesus, be with me today,
And my family
Help me share my faith with them
For all eternity.

76.

Protector of Life

Jesus Lord, protector of life,
To you we humbly pray,
Replace our callousness with fire,
Defending life today.

Take from our hearts all ignorance
All apathy we feel,
Give us the heart to do what's right
And grace to grow in zeal.

You did not make death, O Lord,
You want that all should live.
All life is so precious to you,
The prize of life, you give.

Many rejoice in destroying
That which is beautiful,
Made in your own image,
Creation's pinnacle.

Jesus, O King of Creation,
Our world is filled with strife,
With desire to kill the living,
Protect us, Lord of Life.

77.

Put On Jesus

"Put on Jesus", St. Paul commands,
Like a new suit or shirt.
Purity, love, kindness, too,
Compassion, healing hurt.

Clothe yourself in what Jesus wore,
He's never out of date.
Virtue is always right in style,
While his coming we await.

O Jesus, Lord, please be with us
To give us hope and sight,
That in the darkness we may wear
The armor of your light.

While we're waiting for you, O Lord,
Give us opportunity
To serve and help, indulging not
Ourselves materially.

O Lord, I want to put you on,
To look like you I desire,
Dress me warmly to fight life's cold,
Cover me with your fire.

78.

Render to God

Help me render to you, my God,
All that is truly yours,
You are the source of everything,
Your bounty is outpoured.

You give us life, you give us health,
Our years upon this earth,
Our talents and abilities,
Within, you brought to birth.

I render, Lord, all that I am,
And all that I will be,
I give my faith and love to you,
Your will, please help me see.

You want me to live my life.
With justice, charity,
Upholding with my every breath,
Life's sacred dignity.

79.

Send Me

Let me be your witness, Lord,
You've touched me with your word,
Let me tell to all I meet
What I've seen and heard.

You are the'ternal Son of God,
You died upon the cross,
You gave everything so that
We would not be lost.

Your love reaches out to all
You forgive our sins
You've touched my mind and my heart
And now you dwell within.

You want all the world to know
And everyone to see
What love you have to give to us
O my Lord, send me.

Send me to be your witness, Lord,
To share your vast mercy
Let me share with all who seek,
My Jesus, please send me.

80.

Servant Jesus

Servant Jesus, "on the way"
To give yourself for all,
"Come, and follow after me",
You give to us this call.

The greatest are the least of all,
The first are always last.
Those who love, those who serve,
They are the ones most blest.

You have demonstrated love
For all the world to see.
Your loving service was complete
On the cross of Calvary.

Servant Jesus, you share with us
Your wisdom from above:
"To be great, don't hesitate
To give your life in love."

81.

Servant Lord

Jesus, you are Lord of all,
The greatest of all time,
Yet you demonstrate the truth:
Humble service is sublime.

You redefine true ambition,
It does not dominate.
It does not lord it over one,
It gives, and does not take.

You show us where true greatness is,
Not in power, nor in wealth,
Nor in seeking to be master,
But in the losing of oneself.

Teach us true humility,
Generosity, we implore,
To be a servant, loving all,
Like you, O Servant Lord.

82.

Servant Prayer

Jesus, Lord, O King of Kings,
Eternal God, most strong,
You came with great humility,
And put an apron on.

You are here as one who serves,
You give, not to receive.
Through loving service, we will live,
You call us to believe.

Through our service, we prepare
To meet you face to face.
We will be worthy, if we serve,
To share your holy place.

Let me serve you, Jesus, Lord,
Throughout my whole life long.
I want to follow in your steps,
And put an apron on.

83.

Stewardship Prayer

Jesus make me generous
In my gift to you,
Help me to remember
All my blessings too.

In all my needs and problems
Your grace does now suffice,
So, in my return to you
Help me sacrifice.

The amount is not what matters
In your careful sight,
It's the love which was the value
Behind the widow's mite.

The love within my heart
Is what you want to see,
Behind my gift of money
Given generously.

Help me, Lord, remember
You once paid the price,
Love is the real meaning
Of your sacrifice.

84.

The Beloved Disciple

Jesus, my Lord, you call to me:
"My disciple, come and be.
Believe in me; come and see.
Be my beloved; come, be free."

Risen Jesus, you died for me.
You gave your life upon a tree.
You entered death in agony.
Risen Lord, give life to me.

You call me to be one with you
And to follow faithfully
As your disciple ever true
And to share intimately
Your life, your love, and your joy, too,
A beloved disciple, eternally.

Yes, Jesus Lord, thank you my God,
For allowing me to be
Your follower even to the cross,
To be for others the bearer of
The Gospel triumphing through loss,
As the Disciple whom Jesus loved.

Help me run to your empty tomb,
And be the first to believe,
To have faith without sight,
Your divine blessing to receive,
To shine in darkness as a light
Banishing terror, fear and gloom.

85.

The Face of Jesus

Where can I see the face of Christ
In my world today?
Where is the face of Jesus,
Is he far away?

Where is my compassionate Lord,
Where his merciful eyes,
Where his loving, forgiving smile,
Forged in self-sacrifice?

My Lord is here, with us now,
In our future, too.
I see his face in your loving face.
Jesus is here in you.

He loves us so, he's one with us
I live, now not I,
But Christ dwells within each of us,
With us, he identifies.

We are to show the face of Christ,
His merciful, loving face
His forgiving, tender, caring gaze
Upon the human race.

86.

God's Choice

Jesus, Lord, you are here,
My heart is full today,
You call me and you love me.
Don't let me run away.
Your love for me is so strong,
And yet, so very tender.
Help me to be found by you,
And to you, my life surrender.

Help me to become like you,
Wearing like a garment,
Your sweet wisdom and your love,
You are Love incarnate.
Send me now, O Lord, I pray,
With a faithful vision,
And a heart of love for you,
Help me accept my mission.

To always bring your love to life,
To yours, my will to bend,
To grow in my relationship
With you, who call me "friend".
When I see within your heart
Your love, so unalloyed,
Then you will give to me
Your blessed peace and joy.

87.

The Narrow Gate

Your gate is narrow, difficult,
Hard to get inside,
While the gate to selfishness
And sin is very wide.

Because your entrance means that we
Must give compassionately,
And serve each other well each day,
With loving generosity.

It's so easy to be selfish
And full of arrogance.
But living egoistically
Is really ignorance,

Ignorance of the truths of life
The truth which makes us whole,
Bringing us such happiness,
Healing the hurting soul.

The narrow gate means loving, Lord,
Not giving in to hate.
It means being one with you.
You are the narrow gate.

88.

The Touch

Jesus, Lord, you knew the pain,
You knew the heartache and the shame,
Of the leper, ostracized,
Brutalized and stigmatized,
And everyone who's marginalized.

You bring healing to the heart,
Love's compassion you impart.
Your great empathy is such
That his suffering, though so much,
Finds healing through your very touch.

Touch me, Jesus, touch me too,
So that I may be like you,
With compassion, empathy,
Meeting sorrow with charity,
Growing in my humanity.

Help me respect the dignity,
And the commonality,
That I share with everyone
Touched by the mercy of the Son
Who has for all the victory won.

89.

The Widow's Gift

The widow, Lord, gave all she had;
There was nothing left to give.
She loved you, Lord, with heart and soul,
She shows us how to live.

To live in trust, that you'll take care
Of all we really need.
You are there with grace and peace.
There to protect and feed.

She gave all with joyful heart,
Glad that she could share.
Joy and peace come over us
When we love and care.

Help me to be generous,
In time and talent, too,
And giving of my treasure,
In giving back to you.

A widow poor, but rich in faith,
Beloved in your sight,
Gives the most; gives the best,
In her widow's mite.

90.

To Serve

Serving others is the path
To take in following you.
Jesus, Lord, great Servant King,
May we serve in all we do.

What a paradox, O Lord,
Dominance is futility.
While joy and greatness we will find
In seeking true humility.

Great servant Lord, Jesus Christ,
You won everything in loss.
In death you show the way to life,
You triumphed on the cross.

Help us, Lord. Teach us, Lord.
In us your truth preserve.
Show us, Lord, that to be great
Is to seek only to serve.

91.

True Riches

Jesus, Lord, you are so rich,
The master of everything.
Through you the universe was made,
You are the King of Kings.

But you gave up everything.
You left your throne on high,
And entered our own human world,
In poverty, born to die.

You gave your life upon the cross
In love, for all of us.
You emptied yourself generously,
With grace, magnanimous.

You teach us all, O Lord God,
The meaning of riches true,
Is found in giving from the heart,
Putting love in all we do.

Help us then, dear Lord, today,
To put away all greed,
To think of only serving well,
With trust you'll fill our need.

92.

True Treasure

Set your heart on true treasure,
Not on lesser things.
Not on the material goods of earth,
But what the Spirit brings.

Thieves can steal, moths destroy,
All things pass away.
What endures, what perdures,
What will always stay?

Think of the most important things
That which is durable,
That which lasts without end,
That which is spiritual.

Your love for God is always first,
That will last forever.
Your love for neighbor also abides,
These two will fail you never.

93.

Use It or Lose It

Lord, you lay it on the line,
And we may not have much time.
You've given us so many gifts,
That, if unused, you'll say, to wit,
Use it or lose it.

Don't let fear or laziness
Render my life powerless
In serving you with great trust.
Help me realize that I must
Use it or lose it.

I may not have so much to give,
My gifts may be diminutive,
But I can give them, even still,
And I know well that I will
Use it or lose it.

Jesus, you gave all for me,
Love was nailed up on that tree,
Let love be my motivation.
Help me know if love I ration,
I'll use it or lose it.

94.

Witness Prayer

Jesus Lord, touch my heart,
Touch my spirit too.
Your Gospel, Lord, may I impart
By all I say and do.

Let me be your witness, Lord.
Teach me what to say.
Give me courage and deep love
Enough to show the way.

The way you paved for me, O Lord,
Through my family dear.
They taught by words and by deeds,
Your Gospel I did hear.

May my family learn from me
Faith, love, and justice too.
May I model living faith
To help them follow you.

Help me witness to my faith
To all those who doubt,
At work and in my neighborhood,
To them help me go out.

95.

World On Fire

Jesus, you came to set afire
The earth with all its pain
You want to restore our lives
With faith and love again.

Ignite my heart, O Jesus Lord,
With burning love for you
Fill me with zeal and hopefulness
My heart and soul renew.

Inflame my passion and desire
To build your kingdom, Lord,
To share the Gospel with everyone,
To serve you and adore.

Touch my mind and inner being,
Set my soul ablaze,
With love for you and trust in you,
To give you endless praise.

Use me Jesus, to set aflame
Other hearts as well,
By my faithful witness, Lord.
Within our hearts, come dwell.

96.

"Yes, Lord"

Why do I say "No", my Lord,
When you call me to
Live a better, holier life,
Life lived closer to you?

Sometimes, Lord, I tell you "Yes",
"Yes, I'll do what you will."
But then I disobey so soon,
With deceit, my love I kill.

Hold this sinner in your arms,
Arms that forgive my loss
Of innocence and grace and life,
Arms stretched on a cross.

Help me say "Yes" whene'er you call,
With faith and love long due,
Help me say "Yes" with willing heart,
Saying "Yes" in what I do.

FAITH, HOPE AND LOVE

97.

A New Commandment

Jesus, you call us to love
Just as you love us.
We become like you, Lord,
When we are generous.

To love, I must want the best,
Be willing to sacrifice,
To help another in his need,
Willing to pay the price.

To be like God, this you ask,
You want us to love like him,
Who did not spare his only Son,
To take away our sin.

Love is shown every day
In action and its fruit.
Love is key to happiness,
There is no substitute.

Jesus, Lord of Life and Love,
Be with us today.
Help us to love, as you love us,
Help us, Lord, we pray.

98.

Abba

Our Father dear, you love us so,
You want our happiness,
In this world, and the world to come,
You want nothing less.

You call us all to trust in you,
To trust with all our heart,
That you care and you are here,
Your blessing to impart.

You are "Abba", so close to us,
And we need you so,
You are awesome, powerful,
Your graces always flow.

You are Father to everyone
We are not alone,
You teach us, " Love your family,
So all come safely home."

99.

Be Opened

Jesus, healer of the sick,
Not by magic, not by trick
You bring hearing to the deaf,
The mute now speaks. In joy he wept.

"Be opened" were the words you said,
"Be opened" was the way you led.
"Be opened"; now you speak to me,
"Hear my words, my disciple be"

Help me hear you, truly hear
Help me praise you without fear.
Touch my ears, my mouth and tongue.
Share with me, your victory won,

Won upon the cross of pain,
The cross you suffered for our gain,
There the lance opened up your side,
That our hearts be opened wide.

Opened to receive your love,
Given freely from above.
Opened to your sick, your poor.
Opened to love them all the more.

100.

Blessing or Curse

Lord you offer blessing or curse,
We are the ones who choose.
If we follow your commands,
We/ll win, and never lose.

All is found in the inner self,
In our heart and in our soul,
There we are blessed, or we are cursed,
There we are lost, or whole.

The surface of life looks so good,
But it is incomplete.
It is in your heart and soul,
That peace and joy will meet .

Jesus, help us follow you,
In all of this life's trial,
We want the blessing, not the curse,
Bless us, and stay awhile.

101.

Hurry, Lord

Hurry, Lord, hurry, please.
There is no time to lose.
Send your Spirit into my life,
That your way I may choose.

I have so many vices, Lord,
There's pride and lust and hate.
Send your Spirit; help me change,
I tend to procrastinate.

I put off so many things
I know I should do now.
Change is hard and difficult,
At times, I don't know how.

A mountain you want me to move,
No wonder I put it off,
But if I do not level it,
I know I will be lost.

So help me, Lord, and hurry, please,
So I won't be too late.
With your love and with your grace,
No mountain is too great.

102.

Call to Mercy

Lord of mercy, O Lord of love,
You show us the way.
You see beyond our sins; you see
Gold amidst the clay.

You are so merciful and kind,
You embrace us all,
Forgiving, healing all in need,
"Follow me", you call.

Dear Jesus, help me follow you,
This is the true test,
Can I be blind to others' sins,
And find in them the best.

I know I don't deserve your love,
Nor your gifts to me,
Help me to follow where you lead,
In generosity.

103.

Cana Prayer

Jesus, guest at Cana feast,
Honoring promise, love and peace,
Bring your blessing, never cease,
Change water into wine.

Bless our families with your love,
Send your Spirit like a dove,
Come to them from above,
Change water into wine.

As the Cana wedding guest,
Their union with your presence blest,
Your blessing is now our request,
Change water into wine.

Change our families through the years,
Increase their love through being near,
Give them joy instead of tears,
Change water into wine.

The last was better than the first,
Through the years, quench their thirst
For love and joy in life immersed,
Change water into wine.

Jesus, guest at Cana feast,
Honoring promise, love and peace,
Bring your blessing, never cease,
Change water into wine.

104.

Come to the Banquet

"Come to the banquet" Lord, you invite
All who are poor, without power or might,
The wealthy as well you call to come, too,
Theirs is a hunger filled only by you.

"Come to the banquet, come by my side,
Fill up your hearts, with me abide."
You generously share all that you are,
Your banqueting hall is not very far.

When e're I see, someone who's poor,
Someone who's sick, someone heart-sore,
Someone who's lonely, by life overcome,
Then you invite me, then you say "Come."

"Come with compassion, come and now give,
Only by dying can you really live.
Die to yourself, give of your heart,
Come to my banquet, from me never part."

O Jesus, my Master, I hear your sweet voice,
You call me to share in all of your joys,
In a banquet of love, for all of your friends,
A banquet of life, that will never end.

105.

Come, Spirit

Come, Spirit, Spirit come!
Impale me with your living flame.
Sanctify, unify
Our world, so full of strife and pain.

End our hate, hostility,
Fill our hearts with love Divine.
Our divisions, terminate,
Our souls and hearts now align.

Jesus, you came to make us one,
Your love for us is supreme.
You gave all for us, O Lord,
You came to save, and to redeem.

O touch our hearts, most precious Lord,
With your love uniting,
With holy longing to see your face,
Fill our inner being.

What is heaven yet to come?
What our destiny?
You want us all to share with you
Perfect peace and unity.

106.

Faith

Jesus I believe in you.
Help my unbelief.
Help me trust you more and more,
Lest I come to grief.

To believe is to say "yes"
To what you want of me.
To want to have you in my life,
And now to really see.

To see the truth as it is
With all honesty.
Truth brings joy to my heart,
Your truth will set me free.

Trusting you with all my heart
Trusting you are near.
Trusting that you love me so.
Trust destroys all fear.

Lord Jesus I believe in you.
Come, my fears relieve.
Cast away now all my doubts.
Jesus, I believe.

107.

Find Him

"We want to see Jesus", the visitors said.
"We want to see Jesus. We want to be fed.
Fed with his wisdom, to taste of his bread."

"Where can we find him? Where can he be?
How can we get there? How can we see,
See him, our Savior, who suffered for me?"

In his Word you will find him, in his Word he will be,
In his Word of the Gospel, In his Word you will see.
You will see there his love, and you will be free.

Look for him there in the bread and the wine,
Broken, outpoured, there you will find
The Lord of all Nations, Jesus, Divine.

Are you looking for Jesus to serve and adore?
You can see Jesus in the eyes of the poor.
Find him and love him in the poor and heartsore.

Where are you, Jesus, where can you be?
You will find Jesus in your own family.
Love him and serve him in your family.

We want to see Jesus, we want to be fed.
We want to see Jesus, we want to be led,
To be led to his side who died in our stead.

O Jesus, we love you, our prayer please now hear.
Please never leave us, cast out all our fear.
Help us come closer, O Jesus, be near.

108.

God's Love

Jesus, Lord, you are here,
My heart is full today,
You call me, and you love me,
Don't let me run away.
Your love for me is so strong,
and yet so very tender,
Help me to be found by you,
And to you, my life surrender.

Help me to become like you,
Wearing like a garment,
Your sweet wisdom and your love,
You are Love incarnate.
Send me now, O Lord I pray,
With a faithful vision,
And a heart of love for you,
Help me accept my mission.

To always bring your love to life,
To yours, my will to bend,
To grow in my relationship,
With you, who call me friend.
When I see within your heart
Your love, so unalloyed,
Then you will give to me,
Your blessed peace and joy.

109.

Habits

My habits, Lord, control my life,
And that's not always good.
I often do the things I shouldn't,
And not the things I should.

It's likely I'll take the easy way,
Especially when I'm, stressed,
And I can be so selfish, too,
And prideful, I confess.

Lord, I don't really like the way
That I react at times.
Please help me change my inner self,
For something more sublime.

Give me patience when I'm distressed,
And more compassion, too.
Help me see the real value of
The other's point of view.

But habits can be really good,
If the good we cultivate.
Be with me, Lord, and help me, Lord,
Good habits to create.

110.

Help Me Grow

Jesus, help me grow today
Help me love you more.
Show me the path that I must walk
Please teach me, I implore.

You call us to conversion, Lord,
To turn away from sin,
You offer fullness in our life
You want to dwell within.

Come to me, my Jesus, Lord,
Come to me today,
Fill me with your Spirit, Lord,
Come to me to stay.

Help me trust you and believe,
No matter what may come,
Give me strength to persevere,
My sins to overcome.

Sow your Word within my heart,
Your truth within my mind,
May I be fruitful in my life,
My heart with yours align.

111.

Help Me Trust, Lord

Help me trust in you, O Lord,
Lord of all the earth
You have blessed my life so much,
Richly from my birth.

Help me not rely on wealth
As my security,
You are the source of all blessing,
Even my abilities.

Give me compassion for the poor
I want to follow you,
To make their cause my very own,
With love my life imbue.

Help me trust in you, O Lord
And with your grace comply,
To be always grateful for your gifts,
On your presence to rely.

112.

Hope

Why do some live in fear?
It is, of course, our choice,
If we wish to submit
And not to raise our voice.

To meekly bow beneath the load,
Like beaten beasts of burden.
But that is just a form of death,
Of this, I'm truly certain.

As long as there is life and will,
There is no defeat,
With God's help and his love,
Mercy, justice meet.

Don't give up, just have hope,
Go to any length,
To persevere, to carry on,
Hope is our true strength.

113.

I Am Third

Jesus, be first in my life,
First in all I do.
Help me think of self as last,
And first in loving you.

Let me not live selfishly,
Nor choose a lesser goal.
I want to live life fully, Lord,
And to be truly whole.

You are the Way, the Truth, the Life.
You show me how to live.
You are my model and my joy,
Demonstrating how to give.

Loving Jesus, you are first,
Second are all my friends.
I am third, but my hope is placed
In life that never ends.

114.

I Believe

Jesus, I believe in you
I believe your words are true
"My flesh, real food",
"My blood, real drink"
These words are ever new.

You are really present here
There is nothing we should fear.
We are so deeply loved by you
That you come to us as food.
You're not absent. You are near.

How awesome it is to behold
Your love as it unfolds,
Sharing your divinity
With our poor humanity
My God this food now holds.

My Jesus, Lord, what relief,
Our salvation, you achieve.
Now you make us one with you
Thru Precious Blood, and Body too,
Blessed Savior, I believe!

115.

I Trust You, Lord

Loving Father, be with me when
Things get out of hand.
When I hurt so terribly with
Pain I cannot stand.

Worry sometimes fills up my life,
And my eyes with tears,
Be my strength, my hope, my God,
And remove my fears.

To live in fear is such a shame,
To think that you're not here.
My faith is lacking in your love,
When faith gives way to fear.

O my God, I trust in you,
Help me trust you more.
Be with me when things go wrong.
I trust you, O my Lord.

116.

Joy

There's a secret, how to find,
Now, and not tomorrow,
To truly find the joy of life,
When in painful sorrow.

Pain is just an outside coat,
A fraud, a lie, a sin,
It covers all, and seems all,
It's not the real within.

How could it be, finally,
When within the heart there is,
A spark of hope, stubbornly,
A longing, a thirst, a wish.

Much more than that, there is one,
Who has gone before,
To lead, to steel, to comfort, too,
A heavy cross he bore.

He offered all, surrendering all,
To the one above,
He found joy, in midst of pain,
His joy was found in love.

Give us that love, O Savior dear,
My fears and grief destroy,
Give me love and give me life,
Give me your peace and joy.

117.

Joyful Jesus

Joyful Jesus, you show the way
To live life to the fullest,
And to be so full of joy,
To be what our God willest.

The way you show is simple, Lord,
It's found most every day,
When we're kind and generous
In what we do and say.

You gave all for us in love,
Upon the cross you died
To save us from unending death,
And so with you abide.

In our giving to those in need,
We find gladness and delight.
In walking in your footsteps, Lord,
We walk into the light.

Joyful Jesus, come to us,
Come to us today,
In our caring and our love,
Come to us to stay.

118.

Keep Me Safe

Jesus help me listen
To your words of life.
You are always present
To protect from sin and strife.
For me you paid the price.

Danger lies around me,
Sin of every kind,
Lord, I'm sorely tested,
Safety, help me find,
Conform my will to thine.

Help me to be open
To your voice within,
You whisper in my heart,
To keep me from all sin,
So heaven I might win.

Journey with me, Lord,
Your love to me impart,
Keep me from all evil,
From me never part,
Dwell within my heart.

119.

Live In My Love

My Jesus, Lord, you love us so,
Like the Father has love for you.
"Remain in my love", this you want,
That we share your inner life too.

What mystery in this, my Jesus,
And yet, so real and concrete,
It's all about loving each other,
In loving, it's God that we meet.

But love has so many faces,
It's giving and forgiving too,
Every day as we live our lives,
Generously following you.

Not forgetting your blessings,
Being thankful, especially for all
The wonderful people you give us,
That's how we answer your call.

This is your new commandment.
"Love others as I have loved you."
In obeying, we enter the mystery,
And our lives you create anew.

120.

Loving Enemies

To turn the other cheek, O Lord,
Is pretty hard to do,
When I am hurt, or put upon,
I get mad, revengeful, too.

You ask a lot of me, O God,
To love my enemy,
Doing good when I am hurt,
Forgiving generously.

You don't want me to strike back,
Or to run away.
Courageous love, You want to see,
Without violence, to repay.

Help the other see his fault,
To understand that he
Violates his own self-worth,
When assaulting me.

Jesus, Lord, show me the way,
With mercy ever new,
Repaying hurt and pain with love,
Following after You.

121.

Law Of Love

To live your law is life, o Lord,
It is to follow you
We can choose to live or die
To die or live anew.

To love is how we live your law
To reconcile, to give,
To sacrifice for other's good,
To form relationships.

Never harboring angry thoughts,
Speaking with respect,
Forgiving from the heart when hurt,
That's the ultimate test.

To live a life of chastity,
Not indulging lust,
Respecting persons in our thoughts,
Creating faith and trust.

To love you, Lord, with all my soul,
With love that is heart felt,
This is your great command to us
Love neighbor as oneself.

122.

Mustard Seed Faith

Jesus, Savior, give us faith,
Heartfelt faith in faithful deed.
What power we experience though
Faith be small as mustard seed.

Mustard seed faith, if real and true
Brings peace of mind and soul,
And changes us miraculously.
Life becomes full and whole.

Jesus, touch our lives with faith,
Help us trust in you.
Be our power in daily life.
In grief, be our strength, too.

Jesus, Servant-King and Lord,
May the seeds of our faith grow,
And help the faith of others when
The seeds of faith we sow.

Make us your true servants, Lord,
Sowers of your seed.
Jesus, give us loving faith,
If only small as mustard seed.

123.

New Eyes

Give me, Lord, new eyes to see,
Help me to know you're here.
In life's troubles and its joys,
Help me to feel you're near.

Jesus you are always there,
Even when friends are gone.
You never leave us all alone,
You help us to go on.

Help me see your presence, Lord,
In the beauty of the day.
Let me hear your words of love,
And the truth you want to say.

Reveal yourself in friend and foe,
In laughter and in tears,
Show me how you are close by
And I don't need to fear.

Give me eyes that see the good
Even in the pain,
Give me hope, when all seems lost,
So I may laugh again.

124.

Perfect Love

Only you have perfect love,
Jesus, Savior, Lord.
You alone love perfectly,
You, whom we adore.

Our love is but a shadow here
Of the love that is to come.
When we will rise above the skies
And with you be truly one.

Help us not mistake the truth,
Or think we have it all.
This world is not all there is,
And death is not final.

There is another world for us
Our true and certain home,
To be with you forevermore,
Never to be alone.

So help us all to be detached
From things which will decay,
And to worship you alone,
Not the things that you have made.

125.

Prayer for Hope

The world sometimes seems hopeless, Lord,
Nothing is going right.
Evil seems to be winning out,
Sometimes without a fight.

Hatred and warfare, fear and strife,
The human heart seems dark.
Hopefulness is hard to find
When evil looms so stark.

Help me, Lord, to always believe
The world is in your hands.
Your kingdom will come in due time,
Peace will come to our land.

Give me the wisdom and the love
To bring some hopefulness;
To light a candle rather than
Curse the evil darkness.

126.

Prayer For Inner Strength

Jesus give me courage
When there's conflict in my life.
Never let me waver
In facing moral strife.

Keep me always honest
In the decisions I must make,
Always wanting your will
In the course that I will take.

Let me not be selfish
In following after you.
Help me to be virtuous
In all I say or do.

Strengthen me in conscience,
In moral fortitude.
Give me moral backbone
So that sin I may elude.

Help me understand, Lord,
True morality,
Help me always follow
What you want for me.

127.

Restless

I am incomplete
Unfinished puzzle
Thirsty for more
Egg cooked too soft
Love song without a lover
Novel without conclusion
Sentence without a verb
Body without soul
Words without heart
Love without feeling
Train without an engine
Walking without a destination
In a crowd without friends
At the grocer's without money
In class without a professor
A prayer without God
Come, Lord Jesus!

128.

Salt and Light

Lord, may we be salt for you,
Salt for all to taste,
Transforming all, by loving all
By you, blessed and graced.

Help us to preserve the truth,
Virtue and the good,
May we be salt, helping others to
Live life as they should.

Lord, help us to be light for you,
Light for all to see,
Bringing faith and hope and love,
To the world in captivity.

Captive by hatred, selfishness,
Violence and by greed,
May love and generosity,
enlighten, heal, and free.

Lord, may we be your salt and light,
Give us what we need,
To build your Kingdom here on earth,
To enlighten and to feed.

129.

Seven Gifts

Holy Spirit, come near to us;
Bring to us your gifts,
So we may give our God glory,
And to you, our lives uplift.

Give us wisdom, knowing your will,
Understanding, too,
Teaching what you revealed to us,
Truth that's always new.

Knowledge to help us live our lives
In holiness and joy.
Counsel to make our choices right.
Sin and hate destroy.

Give us the courage that we need
To live our lives aright,
And piety to be close to you,
Righteous, in your sight.

Give us awe before the Father,
He is to us so good,
So powerful and knowing all,
In loving Fatherhood.

Holy Spirit, help us today,
Our sins to overcome.
To give our Father praise and glory
And with His Son be one.

130.

Shepherd Me

Shepherd me throughout my life,
O Lord, who loves me so,
Lead and guide, steer me straight,
Be near where're I go.

Speak to me within my heart.
What do you want of me?
Call me in the still of night,
O Lord, I want to see.

In all that happens, touch my soul,
In all the bad and good,
Jolt, caress, remind me, Lord,
To choose that which I should.

Enter my relationships,
With family and with friend,
In community, touch me.
Corral this sheep, and tend.

131.

Shepherd of My Soul

Shepherd me, O Jesus,
Shepherd me today.
Speak to me, let me hear
What you have to say.

Guide me from all danger, Lord,
The things that hurt or kill,
Guide my life to safety,
Help me do your will.

Hold me in your loving arms,
Speak within my soul.
I will listen carefully,
Your words can make me whole.

There are so many other sounds,
Voices that distract
From your Gospel teaching, Lord,
Voices that attract.

Keep me strong and faithful,
As my life unfolds,
Walk always beside me,
O Shepherd of my soul.

132.

Shepherd Us

Jesus, Lord, we hear your voice,
"Come and follow me.
Come with faith, come with trust,
Have love and live fully."

Shepherd us, Lord, all our life
Never run away
When the wolf comes near to us
Or when from you we stray.

Show us your protection, Lord,
You are the only Gate
To safety, peace and salvation,
In the face of death and hate.

You know our weakness and our fears,
You call us each by name.
You carry us to safety, Lord.
When we are sick or lame.

Good Shepherd of this wayward flock,
When far from you we roam,
Come, and seek us out, O Lord,
And bring us safely home.

133.

Spirit

Come, Spirit, come again,
Impale me with your living flame.
Burn within me with your fire,
Give me faith and true desire.

Desire for you, O holy One,
Desire that soon your Kingdom come.
Desire for peace, for service too,
Desire inspired by only you.

Help me live my life renewed,
With faith and love my soul imbued,
Strengthen and protect my soul,
Give me courage, self-control.

Give me wisdom plentiful,
Virtue incorruptible.
Help me know your peace, your joy,
All my hates and fears destroy.

Spirit, breathe within my soul,
Fill me, teach me, make me whole.
Blow away all sin and death,
Fill me with your Divine Breath.

Spirit, Lord, come energize,
Activate and mobilize,
Use my gifts for your intent,
Make me Lord, your instrument.

Unite, assemble and connect,
Our unity with Christ effect.
Make us one, our lives align,
Join these branches to the Vine.

Come, O Spirit, Spirit come!
Our rebellion overcome.
Move within us, never cease,
Come, O Spirit, give us peace.

134.

Sweet Surrender

Jesus Lord, how can I cope
With the troubles of this life?
It is so hard, so full of pain,
So violent, marked with strife.

All about I see sadness, grief,
This world so plunged in pain.
How can it be? What does it mean?
Will I find peace again?

I know you want us all to live
This life abundantly,
What is the pathway to that goal,
Lord, help me to see.

"Put your life into my hands"
You whisper in my heart.
"Surrender your whole life to me,
My peace I will impart."

"Offer up your pain, my child,
United to my Cross,
Find meaning in the cross you bear,
Strength and hope in loss."

"And always love, no matter what,
Love in all you do.
In love you find the victory,
With love, life is renewed."

135.

Teach Us To Trust

Jesus, help us trust in you,
To trust and to believe.
Mary trusted in God's word
And then she did conceive.

She is a tower, modeling trust
That we can imitate.
She was open to God's will,
A model to emulate.

Joseph, also, did God's will,
He trusted and believed,
When the angel in a dream
Asked that Mary be received.

Give us Joseph's faith and trust,
That our lives may be
Always open to your will,
Following faithfully.

Our world today contains great fear,
But you with us do dwell,
Help us now with faith and trust
To know Emmanuel.

136.

The Better Part

The better part, O Jesus Lord,
Is to sit down at your feet,
To listen closely, within my heart,
To your words so true and deep.

I am so busy with many things,
I have a cluttered soul,
With many concerns and many works.
But I'm empty. Make me whole.

Help me focus on you, O Lord,
Giving you my full attention,
Spending a little time with you.
Bring peace to all my tension.

Instead of running all the time,
Stop me, slow me down,
So I may find you in my life,
And by you, that I be found.

Show me what's important, Lord,
What's worthy of my heart,
What is real and true and good,
Grant me the better part.

137.

The Better Way

Jesus, Lord, you show us the way
To live a loving life,
Whenever we have been hurt,
Even in pain and strife.

Anger, vi'lence self-perpetuate
Time and time again.
They don't accomplish anything
Hate is their dividend.

The much better way is to love,
To forgive the offense,
True, to protest the injustice,
But with non-violence.

Just as violence goes on and on,
Anger will never cease,
Until it finds true forgiveness,
Which is the seed of peace.

Forgiveness and love go on and on,
They self-perpetuate.
They have the power to heal, convert,
They are the better way.

138.

The Eleventh Hour

Lord, It doesn't seem right to me,
When you give the same
To those who work and those who don't
Because late they came.

They didn't work as long as I
Did with sweat and thirst.
How come you treat them the same?
You make the last the first.

Will it be the same some day
When this life is done?
Even though they're last to serve,
They too get salvation?

I know that I can't earn heaven.
Heav'n I'm not owed.
It is all your gift to us,
Given with love untold.

You reward the first and last.
Your love is great pow'r.
Saving the first and those who come
At the eleventh hour.

139.

The Good Shepherd

Jesus, Shepherd of my soul,
You know us all by name.
You lead and guard and sanctify,
Hold close all those in pain.

You know your sheep and we know you,
We know your deep compassion.
You care, and offer forgiveness,
For our sins of degradation.

You readily leave the ninety-nine
To search for one who's lost.
I, too, having wandered off,
Was found at such great cost.

When I entered death's valley,
And from your path diverged,
You lay down your life for me,
You are the Good Shepherd.

O Good Shepherd, be with us now,
Protect us as your own.
And when our life on earth is done,
Lead us safely home.

140.

The Pearl

Lord, I long within my heart,
I am yet to be fulfilled.
I seek, I want what I don't have,
My heart will not be stilled.

What is that treasure buried deep
For which I'd give my soul?
What is that pearl of such great price
I need to make me whole?

Money, power, fame are things
Material which I pursue.
But they don't fill the void within.
That can be filled by only you.

You are my treasure, You my pearl,
Your Kingdom I desire,
Born within me by your hand.
It is you who sparked this fire.

I give you all that I possess
My life, my heart, my all,
Fill me with your love, your life.
Fill my empty soul.

141.

To See You

To see you, Jesus, face to face,
You, my Lord, my friend.
I have loved you all my life;
On you my life depends.

I thirst for you, like wind blown sand.
With you, I want to be.
Without faith, let me see you;
You are life itself to me.

Death is so cold, so powerful.
It makes life seem a joke.
But you destroy death's cruelty;
You are my only hope.

I know too well my world will end.
I know that I will die.
But I believe in you, my Christ;
To you my soul will fly,

Fly above this vale of tears,
Soar beyond the grave.
Death, you have no victory,
My life, my Christ did save.

Jesus, guide me, show me how
To keep life's goal in sight.
Enlighten my way, so that I may
Walk in endless light.

142.

To Whom Shall We Go?

Lord, to whom shall we go?
We don't want to leave.
We may not fully understand,
But Lord, we do believe.

Fill us with your light and truth,
Feed us with your word.
Give us your body and your blood,
With love, our lives come gird.

Send us forth to bring your love
To a world that is forlorn,
Send us to bring your peace and joy,
To those tossed in life's storms.

In this sacred bread and cup
You come to energize
Our lives with your own strength and pow'r,
So that we may arise

To bring your truth into our world,
So blind and incredulous,
And bring you to all those in need.
We're your servants, Lord, send us.

143.

Tough Love

Jesus Lord, help me to care enough
For wrong to lay bare,
Exposing the truth, if I dare,
Give me tough love.

Help me, Lord, to take a stand,
When all around seem to band
Against the welfare of the land,
Give me tough love.

When my neighbor is in trouble,
Living a life that is double,
Headed now for waste and rubble,
Give me tough love.

You made us, Lord, our neighbor's keeper,
To live and grow in love that's deeper
To climb the hill a little steeper,
Give us tough love.

144.

Truth Rejected

Jesus, Lord, I didn't hear
What you had to say,
I didn't want to see the truth
And have to change my ways.

You didn't come yourself, O Lord,
I would have listened then.
Instead, you sent a messenger,
You sent to me my friend.

He told the truth. What was real,
I couldn't accept at all.
The truth hurt. What did he know?
And so I built a wall.

I rejected truth that day,
True friends are really few.
And like the folks in Nazareth
I rejected you.

You wanted them to change, O Lord,
As you wanted me,
If I had only listened then,
The truth would set me free.

145.

Ultimate Values

Teach me Lord how to live,
What to value in my life.
Show me the way, guide me today,
Fix in my heart what is right.

I get distracted by some things
Material which I own,
Or things I want which I don't have
Sometimes get overblown.

Fame and power, money too,
Are things which I pursue.
But are they the things which last,
Fulfilling my life through?

To love you, Lord, must be first,
In finding happiness,
And loving others as best I can,
Herein lies the test.

When I die the things I love
Will not go with me.
Only my relationships
Find immortality.

146.

Universal Love

Jesus you revealed that we
Are infinitely loved by God,
Men and women, children too,
No matter how we're flawed.

All are precious in your sight,
None is superior.
All are called to be with you,
None is inferior.

You reach out to all of us,
Especially the weak and small,
The born and unborn little ones,
Lord, you love them all.

Change our hearts and minds, O Lord,
We love to dominate,
We look down with arrogance,
We kill and discriminate.

Help us to love all on earth
As they are loved by you,
May we reflect your divine plan
By what we say and do.

147.

We Walk By Faith

Jesus, Lord, we walk by faith,
We have confidence
That you are here and you are near
With your divine presence.

You ask us all to trust in you,
In your promise true,
That as we face life's challenges,
You will bring us through.

To have faith in you, Jesus God,
Always to choose the right
No matter what the challenge, Lord,
That you, with us, abide.

Give us wisdom, and courage too,
To say "Yes" to you,
When faced with choices difficult,
Our life with faith imbue.

Don't let doubt disturb our faith,
Our hearts with love ignite,
Be with us Lord, and help us, Lord,
To walk by faith, not sight.

148.

Welcome Him

Joseph welcomed Jesus
As his very own.
When the angel told him
This is God's own son.

He showed great compassion
And great trust in God.
And when this child was born
He was over awed.

This child of God, now his child,
To love and to care for,
His heart was open to God's plan,
He could not love him more.

Joseph is our model,
Whom we imitate.
We are called to welcome,
And to celebrate,

Those who are unwanted,
Unwelcome and despised,
Those who need our love,
And our sacrifice.

When we welcome others
With kindness ever true,
Then, Lord God Almighty,
Then we welcome you.

149.

What Is Love Like?

Jesus Lord, what is love like?
Teach us what it means.
How can we be more like you,
Who embody love supreme?

"Love seeks to give, not just receive,
It sees the others' tears.
It sacrifices willingly,
To calm another's fears."

"Love is bold, and lets no fear,
Prevent its doing good,
It does what's right even when
It is misunderstood."

"Love doesn't quit when difficult.
It perseveres throughout.
Love is gentle, yet so strong,
It does not give in to doubt."

"Love is giving, merciful,
It listens to God's call.
It's not stingy, miserly.
It's willing to give all."

150.

Your Law

To live your law is life, o Lord,
It is to follow you
We can choose to live or die
To die or live anew.

To love is how we live your law
To reconcile, to give,
To sacrifice for other's good,
To form relationships.

Never harboring angry thoughts,
Speaking with respect,
Forgiving from the heart when hurt,
That's the ultimate test.

To live a life of chastity,
Not indulging lust,
Respecting persons in our thoughts,
Creating faith and trust.

To love you, Lord, with all my soul,
With love that is heart felt,
This is your great command to us
Love neighbor as oneself.

SIN AND FORGIVENESS

151.

Friend of Sinners

Friend of sinners, sinless one,
Never the sinful do you shun.
No matter how great may be the sin,
You're always ready to take me in.

You know our hearts, our weakness, too,
You want to cleanse our lives anew.
When I my failings do confess,
I know your love and forgiveness.

How can I with anger judge
My neighbor, and myself not budge
To change my heart and evil ways,
Beneath your knowing, tender gaze?

Let me hear your words so kind;
Etch these words upon my mind:
"On Calvary your sins I bore.
Go, my friend, and sin no more."

152.

Good and Evil

Lord, in my world I see both
Good and evil things.
What should I do, how should I feel,
When life evil brings?

Should I judge someone else's heart,
And condemn the bad?
Should I exclude them from my life,
Expel the evil-clad?

But I can't read another's heart,
Much less know their mind.
If someone looked within me,
Would only good they find?

Help me grow in holiness,
So I might be like you,
Loving even sinners, Lord,
Hoping to help a few.

When evil darkness overwhelms,
Let me not curse the night,
Giving in to hoplessness,
Instead, a candle, light.

153.

Cleansing the Temple

Jesus, Lord, so full of fire,
You drove the sellers out.
It was zeal for God's own house
Behind your fearsome shout.

"My Father's house, a house of prayer,
Which you have desecrated.
You exploit God's own poor,
The devout you have frustrated.

Lord, we are God's temple now
As members of your Body,
God in You and You in us,
In us dwells God Almighty.

In your zeal, cleanse this house
From selfishness and sin.
Share with us your zealous heart
That we be cleansed within.

Help us, Lord, to understand,
To appreciate just how
Great is your own love for us,
We are your temple now.

154.

Come Out

"Lazarus, come out!" were your words
Your command to him,
Four days dead, there was a stench,
It smelled like death did win.

What pow'r was there in your word,
The very pow'r of God,
Creating the stars by a word.
Your friend lives, over-awed.

"Do you believe," you ask us now,
"Do you believe in me?"
Yes, O Lord, we do believe,
Give us eyes to see.

It is our sins that bury us,
In that cold, dark tomb.
Call us out with your mighty word,
Destroy death and doom.

"Come out, come out, come out now!
Live life ever new!"
Give the command so we may stand,
And live fore'er with you.

155.

Divine Mercy

Merciful Jesus, risen Lord,
Your mercy is divine.
Your love goes out to everyone
And lasts throughout all time.

Our sins are great and terrible
Begging wrath from above.
But there is nothing greater, Lord,
Than your infinite love.

Our lives are filled with suffering,
Loss, sickness, and pain.
But we survive because, O God,
Your mercy falls like rain.

Terror, war, and violence,
These we must endure.
We don't despair; we have hope.
The vict'ry you assure.

We trust in you, Jesus, Lord,
Your love fills earth and sea,
You forgive us all, you bless us all,
You are Divine Mercy.

156.

Divine Teacher-Exorcist

Jesus, Lord, Teacher Divine,
Show me the way, your truth sublime.
Lead me, and guide me. Show me your light.
Sometimes I'm blind. Please give me sight.

Teach me what love is, how to forgive.
Teach me compassion, to fully live.
Show me true values, to rightly choose
The good and the true, how best to serve you.

Cast out my demons, Divine Exorcist,
The demon addiction and my selfishness.
Sometimes I'm possessed by egoism,
Given to pleasure, materialism.

If I make you first, O my dear God,
No more demons my soul will maraud.
If in my heart I enthrone you,
There you save me, and evil subdue.

Teach me to trust you with all my heart
The grace to surrender please now impart.
Help me to work with all of my might,
Trusting that you will make all things right.

Come, my dear Jesus, come, never part.
Come with compassion, come fill my heart.
You are my Teacher, Exorcist, Friend,
Come, give me your life, that will never end.

157.

Heal Me, Lord

Dear Lord, my God, I am in need
Of healing for my soul.
I feel lost; I feel ashamed.
Come and make me whole.

Give me the courage to admit
The wrong that I have done.
Forgive my pride, I cannot hide.
Humility, I have none.

Give me the strength to resist
Opposition when it comes
To my desire to heal my soul.
My spirit, pride does numb.

O Jesus, Lord of my whole life,
I praise and thank you Lord.
You give me healing and new life.
My soul you now restore.

158.

Help Me Repent

Jesus, come into my life,
Come into my heart.
Fill me with your precious love,
Come, and ne'er depart.

With Mary, help me long for you.
Hope had filled the earth,
And Mary longed so fervently,
Waiting to give birth.

But I am such a sinner, Lord,
To sin I do consent.
Move my heart of hearts, O God,
Move me to repent.

Fill me with sorrow for my sin,
For my aberrations,
Forgive me in your Sacrament
Of Reconciliation.

Pardon my sin and wrongdoing,
With mercy you have won,
On the cross of Calvary,
Come, Lord Jesus, Come.

159.

Make Me Ready

Jesus, make me ready
For when you come to me.
Help me to change my life
For when your face I'll see.

Help me be more faithful
In my love for you,
Make me less material,
Less worldly centered, too.

Lead me to repentance
For when I turn away,
Send your Holy Spirit
When you, I disobey.

Help me live a loving life
Of kindness, peace and joy,
Direct my path to justice,
Your Word, help me employ.

O, I long for you, my Lord.
Send me your holy grace,
That I might change today my life,
And someday see your face.

160.

One More Chance

Thanks, dear Jesus, for your love,
Always ready to give and grant
Your forgiveness when I sin.
You give me one more chance.

One more chance to try again,
Merciful pardon you always grant
To your prodigal, coming home.
You give me one more chance.

Patience, Lord, you show to me
When I rave and rant.
You know with grace that I can change,
You give me one more chance.

With grace and unconditional love,
With your gifts, my life enhance,
Jesus, Lord, so good to me,
To give me one more chance.

161.

Prayer For Battle

O Lord, our God, victorious King,
Be with me today
Help me to fight the Good Fight, Lord,
In all I do and say.

The enemy lurks close to me
He is, oh, so near.
Help me to be on my guard,
With me, O God, be here.

He tempts me to use my power
To manipulate and lie,
To seek only what I want,
And allow my love to die.

Come, O Jesus, be my shield.
Strengthen my soul within,
Keep me loyal, faithful, true,
Don't let me fall in sin.

Fill me with strength, spiritual,
I am, oh, so frail,
Live within me, gracious Lord,
With you I cannot fail.

162.

Prayer of the Sinner

Merciful Lord, have mercy on me.
My head is bowed and bent is my knee.
Jesus, my Savior, I love and adore,
You are my God, Redeemer and Lord.

I know in my heart, my sins have hurt you
In what I have done, and failed to do.
I need you, my God, bring peace to my strife,
I need you, my Jesus, each day of my life.

You are my Lord, Creator of all,
I ponder your greatness in wonder and awe.
I am so small, so needy and poor,
Forgive me, my Jesus, whom I adore.

My faults and sins today I can see,
Help me repent in humility.
Be with me, Jesus, I cry aloud,
Have mercy on me, a sinner, O God.

163.

Repent and Believe

Jesus, Lord, I turn away,
From your holy face.
I set my heart not on the good,
But on the crass and base.

You call me to repent, O Lord,
To turn away from sin.
You ask me to reform my life,
And not let Satan win.

Fully to believe in you
Means to now embrace
All that you want of me,
Surrendering to your grace,

Your grace to all sin resist
Satan to defy
Committing not to self indulge
But the self deny.

Jesus Lord, you are my God,
Savior, Redeemer too.
Draw me to yourself, O Lord,
I give myself to you.

164.

Sweet Temptation

Sweet temptation next to me,
Lord, help me to resist,
It looks so good to me right now,
Your help I need enlist.

I am so weak at times like this,
I give in so easily,
It doesn't seem so bad to me,
To stretch morality.

O why do things which are so bad
Seem to me so good?
Why do I want to do the bad,
And not the things I should?

Jesus, Lord, give me strength,
To my aid, please hasten,
Empower me within my will,
To say "no" to sweet temptation.

165.

The Flood

There's a flood that threatens my life,
A flood that's caused by sin.
The waters flow so powerfully,
That death might surely win.

I'm sinking now, I am afraid,
Earthly things weigh me down
Pleasure and pride are my millstone.
I fear that I will drown.

Habits of sin are so engrained,
I cannot now break free.
I am so lost and overcome,
Who will rescue me?

My Jesus, take me in your boat,
To safety my path pave,
You are the Captain of my ship,
Please come, my life to save.

With you the flood will now recede,
As with Noah, long ago.
You are my Savior, Lord and King,
I rejoice seeing your rainbow.

THE CROSS

166.

Daily Crosses

O Jesus, you invite us all
To come and follow you,
In taking up our daily cross,
Whether old or new.

The cross you carried long ago
Was harsh and full of pain.
This cross you bore for love of us,
Your loss becomes our gain.

All the crosses which we will bear,
They bring us close to you,
One with you in your offering
Our love and our life, too.

Today, may my cross be prayer
Offered up sincerely,
For the welfare of all of those
Whom I love so dearly.

O Jesus, hanging from your cross,
You demonstrate the way
To offer up a heart of love,
To offer every day.

167.

Friday's Love

Jesus, Lord, how great your love
Poured out upon the cross.
You gave yourself totally,
Our gain has meant your loss.

Jesus, Savior, racked with pain,
My sins you did atone,
Deserted by your closest friends,
Hanging there alone.

Draw me, Jesus, close to you.
Let me share your pain.
I offer you my very life;
To die to self is gain.

I wish to take my daily cross,
And follow after you.
I offer all I am and have,
Help me be ever true.

Jesus, crucified for me,
Preceeding me across
This world of joy and suffering,
Help me put love into my cross

168.

Give Glory

Jesus, Lord, you gave the glory
To the Father, Lord of all
In your death upon the cross
You reversed Adam's fall

You said "yes" to the Father
Coming to us from above
Showing us how much He loves us
Through your gift of perfect love.

He did not spare you, his own Son
In pain and sorrow you were bathed,
So that we might be forgiven
And that we might all be saved.

The Father then, gave you glory,
Raising you up from the dead,
Giving you your risen splendor
Here with us in cup and bread.

Jesus help us give you glory,
Glory to the Father, too.
Help us live life to the fullest
Becoming what you want us to.

Full of Faith and full of love,
Fulfilling all possibility
That in us you created,
In our being, to give you glory

169.

My Cross

Jesus Lord, you show us how
To carry the cross each day,
"Carry it with love and faith.
Follow me. I am the Way."

I'm tempted, Lord, to say "no".
From my cross, I might run.
Help me say instead with you,
"Father, your will be done."

Help me understand your way.
Reveal it from above,
The real meaning of the cross
Carried with faith and love.

To the fullest help me live.
Give me joy in all I do.
Be one with me in my cross,
And give me life with you.

170.

Seven Last Words

"FATHER, FORGIVE THEM; THEY KNOW NOT WHAT THEY DO."

Jesus, my Lord, my God, my all,
You died upon a tree.
There you gave all the love you had,
You died in agony.

Jesus, Lord, it was my sin, too,
That nailed you cruelly.
It was from sin and selfishness,
You came to set me free.

We have all sinned and turned away;
You wanted but to bless.
"Forgive them, Father", was your prayer.
In you is forgiveness.

We know not, Jesus, what we do,
Such great perversity.
Yet, you respond to all our sins,
With generosity.

"THIS DAY YOU WILL BE WITH ME IN PARADISE"

Remember me, O Jesus Lord,
Remember me, my King.
Do not forget; into my life,
Your life and Kingdom bring.

I feel like nothing, O my Lord,
My life is not worth much.
Yet, I cling to you with trust,
I need your grace, your touch.

Be with me, Lord, be with me now.
Come, and fill my soul.
Take notice of my contrite heart.
I am so lost, so low.

You died for me upon the cross.
For us you paid the price.
Your words to Dismas, speak to me:
"Be with me in Paradise."

WOMAN, BEHOLD YOUR SON; BEHOLD YOUR MOTHER"

Mother, Mary, please pray for me.
Forgive what I have done.
I too have caused such misery
For you and for your Son.

You had to stand beneath the cross,
You watched his life depart,
You held his body in your arms.
A sword did pierce your heart.

Dear Mary, now behold your son.
I give you now my love.
O mother, now be close to me.
Forgive me from above.

Now draw me closer to your heart,
Let me be closer still.
Help me to know a mother's love,
With love, my heart come fill.

"MY GOD, MY GOD, WHY HAVE YOU FORSAKEN ME?"

The prophet's words are now proved true:
"They've numbered all my bones."
Where is my God? Where is he now?
You must meet death alone.

Where are your friends, disciples, Lord?
They have abandoned you.
Only stay the women and John.
I have deserted, too.

Alone you now must face the end,
The thorns, the cross, the rod,

You cry out in dark emptiness,
"Where are you, O my God?"

Silence only returns your cry.
Comfort, you have none.
Like all of us who feel alone,
With us, you are one.

"I THIRST"

Fountain of living water, pure,
You do not count the cost.
You who quench our thirst for life,
You thirst upon the cross.

You thirst while hanging in the sun;
Your bleeding back is arched.
You slowly die in agony;
Your mouth and throat are parched.

O Jesus Lord, you thirst for me;
You think of others first.
You desire our salvation, Lord.
It's for our souls you thirst.

I am thirsty too, my God,
My heart, my life renew.
Help me to understand, O Lord,
My thirst is thirst for you.

"FATHER, INTO YOUR HANDS I COMMEND MY SPIRIT"

It is so hard, so difficult,
Pain, and abandonment,
You are one with all who will know
Hurt, loss, and bereavement.

You see through all the ages, Lord,
The poor, the blind, the lame,
Those who suffer within themselves,
You know well our pain.

You show us now the way, O Lord,
With trust and faith you stand.
You entrust your life, your fate,
Into God's loving hands.

"Your will be done, O Lord, my God!"
I also join your prayer.
I give to you my spirit, Lord,
Into your loving care.

"IT IS FINISHED"

Is it pride or just relief we hear?
"It is finished" your last words.
You sigh your last upon the cross.
Your death seems so absurd.

You are th'eternal Lord of Life,
Son of God and King of Kings.
Though you die a shameful death
Your end is our beginning.

Where you finish, we begin.
You give to us your light.
We are to do your work on earth,
To brighten darkest night.

Help us Lord, be near us Lord.
Without you we will fall.
But with you joined to us on earth,
We too will finish all.

171.

The Cross

O Jesus, Lord, now crucified,
Cruelly hanging on the cross,
What mystery it is to know
Our gain has meant your loss.

What cruelty to crucify!
What inhumanity.
What pain our sins do signify.
What love is on that tree!

You knew what lie ahead for you.
Others were crucified.
You knew what agony and hurt
Would come before you died.

Lord, you cared more for all of us,
More than you feared this end.
You gave all; you left this, our earth.
The Spirit now you send.

The Spirit makes us one with you,
In love and saving pow'r.
We, O Christ, belong to you.
We are yours. Your cross, ours.

172.

What Is My Cross?

What is the cross, my Jesus Lord,
That you have picked for me?
How shall I follow in your steps,
And what shall my cross be?

Will it be heavy, hard to bear?
In pain will my life lead?
Will I say "yes", and carry on,
With love will I proceed?

Or will my cross be found in this:
To watch another's pain?
Will my cross be to help someone
To not live in vain?

It's love whereby I follow you,
No matter what life brings.
Love in living, love in giving,
From generous heart will spring.

173.

Your Cross

Your Cross–your pain–your death,
Jesus, you endure for me.
You gave all in total love,
You die to set me free.
You pour out the cup of wine,
The wine is your blood, red.
Your body hangs in agony,
Broken–Bloody–Dead.
Forgive me, Lord, forgive my sins,
I have turned away
In sin and selfishness, O God,
From you, O Lord, I stray.
My sin has caused your death, your pain,
My sin is selfishness,
I do not love as I should love,
I dwell in pride, self-centeredness.
I give in to every whim,
I follow pleasure, material gain.
My gods are money, power, lust,
My gods are your pain.
"Forgive them, Father", is your prayer,
You greet hate with love.
You give in death eternal life,
Freely, from above.
O Jesus, how great is your love,
You are hung upon a tree.
You have emptied yourself, Lord,
You give your life for me.
Give me faith and help me love,
Show me, Lord, your way.
Do not die in vain, O God,
Save me, with me stay.
Take my heart, my life, O Lord,
I give myself to you.
As you have given all for me,
Take all that I am, too.
Your cruel death delivers me,
You found me when I was lost.
I love you, Lord, with all my heart.
I kiss your feet, your cross.

174.

And Jesus Wept

"And Jesus wept," the Gospel tells,
At Laz'rus' death, your friend.
And when you saw his sisters' tears,
With grief, your heart did rend.

Human Jesus, you're just like me,
You feel our loss and pain.
And when sorrow might fill our hearts,
You feel it, just the same.

Jesus, you are the Son of God,
Divine Lord, source of life.
You raised Lazarus from the dead,
Raise us from grief and strife.

O Jesus, Lord, come resurrect.
Bring to us hope, and more;
Faith and peace bring to us, your friends,
O Lord, whom we adore.

Your risen life with us you share,
What marv'lous mystery
Your tears, and ours, are tears of joy,
You share eternity.

175.

Catch Me, Lord

Stretch your hand, and catch me when
I'm lost in wind and wave.
When I am overwhelmed by fear,
Protect me, Lord, and save.

With my hand in yours, I'm safe
From all hurt and harm.
Hang on to me, help me trust
You'll save me through the storm.

Sometimes the dangers are so great,
Alone, I sometimes feel.
Bleeding, bruised, I will survive
With you to catch and heal.

Stretch your hand and catch me, Lord,
When trouble's at my door.
When in the storms of life, I fear,
Help me trust you more.

176.

Child of God

We grieve today in our loss.
We mourn what might have been;
Our hopes leave us unfulfilled.
O God, our souls now mend.

We come today to say goodbye
To one we never met,
But our hearts are full of love,
For one we'll ne'er forget.

But in the midst of our pain,
We also know real joy,
For life is never truly gone.
Life, you can't destroy.

This little person now lives on.
She lives where from she came,
Lives in perfect, endless joy.
This child, you did reclaim.

O Jesus giver of our life,
Let this child fully live
In perfect love and joy and peace,
Life eternal, to her now give.

And grant, dear Lord, one day to us
That in our arms we hold
This precious little child, so sweet,
Our hearts, with love untold.

177.

Divine Healer

Jesus, heal me in my blindness,
Help me to really see
You in all who suffer,
And that you dwell with me.

Heal me in my lameness, Lord,
Help me now to run,
To jump with joy and hope in you,
My fears to overcome.

I am leprous too, O Lord,
In my sinfulness.
Cleanse me with your pardon, Lord,
Grant me sweet forgiveness.

I am mute and deaf, O Lord,
Let me speak and hear,
To listen to your words, O Lord,
To speak without my fears.

Come and heal my poverty
With your Gospel words,
Give me the true treasure, Lord,
Plant it with me, inward.

178.

Good and Evil

Lord, in my world I see both
Good and evil things.
What should I do, how should I feel,
When life evil brings?

Should I judge someone else's heart,
And condemn the bad?
Should I exclude them from my life,
Expel the evil-clad?

But I can't read another's heart,
Much less know their mind.
If someone looked within me,
Would only good they find?

Help me grow in holiness,
So I might be like you,
Loving even sinners, Lord,
Hoping to help a few.

When evil darkness overwhelms,
Let me not curse the night,
Giving in to hopelessness,
Instead, a candle, light.

179.

Prayer In Time of Trouble

Jesus, Lord, the world seems dark,
Terror, war, famine too,
Evil looms so menacingly,
Threatening all the good we do.

We need hope, we need your grace,
Please help us in our need,
Come, Lord Jesus, come with power,
In word and mighty deed.

Help us put away our fears,
They are of no avail.
You have promised to your church,
Hell's gates will not prevail.

You are Lord, our mighty God,
We place our trust in you.
You are the Savior of the world,
We believe, and love you too.

180.

The Winds and Waves Obey

Jesus, Lord, you are our hope,
In darkest night, our day.
Even in the violent storm,
The winds and waves obey.

Jesus, you are Lord and God.
In our fragile boat you stay.
When we lift our hearts to you,
The winds and waves obey.

Jesus, I give all to you;
Do not turn away.
Take all I am, and please demand
The winds and waves obey.

My heart is troubled and upset,
My worries heavy weigh.
But I know at your command,
The winds and waves obey.

When I trust in you, O God,
Night becomes as day.
You reverse all tragedy,
The winds and waves obey.

181.

Triumphant Cross

Victorious Christ, we adore,
O triumphant cross,
You bring life to us through death,
Gain through pain and loss.

What paradox there is in life,
What awesome mystery!
The first are last, the last are first,
Love only is the key.

Love unselfish, love that's pure,
Love unconditional
Dies to self, yet brings forth life,
Undying life eternal.

Jesus, loving Savior, Lord,
Without you, we are lost.
Be with us, and may we share
The triumph of your cross.

EUCHARIST

182.

Thursday Love

Jesus, Lord of Life, my Lord,
You gather with the twelve.
You share the Paschal meal with them
Before your life's outpoured.

That night when you broke the bread,
It was your body, Lord,
The next day to be broken, too.
With your body, we are fed.

You come in form of Bread and Wine,
You nourish us, O Lord.
Our food and drink, your flesh and blood,
You share your life divine.

You kneel down and wash our feet,
The meaning you reveal,
In Eucharist which we now share,
Love and service meet.

You are Manna from above,
You are life and freedom, Lord,
You show us how to serve and give,
You teach unselfish love.

183.

Corpus Christi

What mystery we celebrate,
The mystery of your love!
In Eucharist we eat your flesh
And we drink your blood.

Your sacrifice on Calvary
You bring to us today,
Your gift of love, your gift of self,
With us forever stay.

We now offer ourselves, too,
O Jesus, saving Lord.
One with you we give our life,
In your blood outpoured.

Renew with us your covenant,
Sealed with your blood red.
We are yours forevermore,
With your flesh we are now fed.

Corpus Christi, Body of Christ,
Blood of him who died,
We live for you, O Jesus Lord,
Who for us was crucified.

184.

Emmaus Lord

O Lord Jesus, at Emmaus,
Your presence you reveal.
You, Lord, are really present at
The Eucharistic meal.

Speak to us in scripture,
In Holy Words once said.
We encounter you through faith,
In the breaking of the bread.

Change our disillusion,
Destroy all doubt and fear,
Open both our eyes and hearts,
Knowing you are here.

Jesus, risen Savior,
Come be with us today.
You walk with us throughout our lives,
May we recognize you, we pray.

185.

I'm Hungry

I'm hungry, Lord, and unfulfilled,
I'm looking for something more
Than what I find in this world,
To make my spirit soar.

Feed me, Lord, with your Word,
Your thoughts restore my youth.
They can feed my inner soul,
Your words of life and truth.

Without your Word, I cannot know
Your love, your will for me,
Help me devour your every word,
Help me, Lord, to see.

But your Word is not enough,
To feed my starving soul,
Give me your Body and your Blood,
These will make me whole.

Your flesh, your blood, this you give
To nourish and renew,
Love is the meaning, your love for me,
My life, your love imbue.

I'm hungry, Jesus, come to me,
Feed me, quench my thirst,
In this food and drink from heav'n,
My soul, come now immerse.

186.

Sacrament Divine

O what wondrous mystery
This Eucharist, O Lord,
You give your body as our food,
Your blood which you outpoured.

Your offering of self, O Lord,
To the Father up above,
Is present in this Eucharist.
We join your gift of love.

As we eat this Bread of Life,
And drink this Sacred Cup,
Eternal life you promise us.
With joy, you fill us up.

You come to us as food and drink,
In the form of bread and wine,
You make us one with you fore'er,
O Sacrament Divine.

187.

The Body And Blood Of Christ

O wondrous mystery of life
That casts out fear and dread,
That feeds and nourishes our lives,
Our food is Living Bread.

O Bread from Heaven, Manna new,
Manna, gift from God,
Our food and drink, Christ's flesh and blood,
We worship you in awe.

We adore, we kneel, we pray,
Jesus, you are near.
In love you come to nourish us,
Jesus, you are here.

You come as food and drink, O Lord,
To comfort and refresh,
One with you, we drink your blood,
With love we eat your flesh.

O mystery inscrutable,
O mystery divine,
The Word made Flesh is now our Guest
In common bread and wine.

O Sacrament of Love Divine,
You are the Prince of Peace,
Bring peace into my heart and world,
With this most holy feast.

Unite us to each other, Lord,
As we are bound to you,
Bind our hearts and souls in life,
As one, our lives renew.

You give to us your body, Lord,
But many go hungry.
In this world of pain and want,
May we your body be.

Help us love and give and serve,
To feed as we are fed,
May our hearts be changed, O Lord,
In the Breaking of the Bread.

O Wondrous Sacrament of Life,
With hope our hearts imbue,
Hope to triumph, hope to share
Eternal life with you.

188.

Two Tables

You set before us two tables,
Two tables offering bread
To feed and nourish, giving life,
From life's true fountainhead.

One table is your Holy Word,
The scriptures feed our souls
With truth and hope, true nourishment.
This food will make us whole.

The other table, like the first
Feeds our inner being,
Your flesh, your precious blood, O Lord,
Your love for us undying.

O Lord, what sacred mystery
You share with us today,
Within this Eucharist, this Mass,
O blessed be this day!

Two tables form such bounty, Lord,
Just so that we might live
Forever in your grace and peace.
Eternal life you give.

ADVENT

189.

Advent Challenge

Advent's here, O Jesus, Lord,
Time to realize
How I love you, give you glory,
And how I compromise.

I want to prepare my heart for you,
To celebrate your birth,
To give honor and glory, Lord,
To always make you first.

But I often make mistakes,
I choose lesser things,
Instead of glorifying you,
I serve other kings.

They are good things, but lesser things,
Above you, these I place.
I can be so selfish, Lord, and
Resist your sweet, sweet grace.

This advent, season of rebirth,
Help me to prepare,
To celebrate incarnate love,
And all my faults lay bare

I want to give you glory, Lord,
To you honor bring,
The main thing, is make the main thing,
Always the main thing.

190.

Advent Jesus

Advent Jesus, come to us,
Come now in joy and peace,
As we prepare for your birthday,
Don't let your blessings cease.

We recall when you first came,
A child, O Divine Guest.
What wonder and what mystery,
The Word of God made Flesh!

We know that you will come again
In glory, at the end,
The end of time, or at my death,
When to you I will ascend.

But the greatest mystery
Is in your coming now,
Through faith and Sacrament and love
To your Body Mystical.

Come, Lord Jesus, come today,
Come, with your vict'ry won,
Come into my heart and life,
Come, Lord Jesus, Come!

191.

Advent Joy

Jesus, you are Advent Joy,
We all rejoice today.
You fill our lives with hopefulness
As we meet you on the way.

You have come in history,
You show that we can trust,
A baby born, a man, a cross,
How greatly God loves us.

You are here with us now
In prayer, in Sacrament,
In your Word, and in the poor,
You are heaven sent.

You will come one day to us,
At the end of life we'll see,
And know the joy of perfect love,
And live eternally.

My Advent joy will never end
No matter what life brings,
Even though tears I shed,
With you my heart sings.

192.

Advent Prayer

O come to us, O Jesus, come,
Come to us today.
Your Advent into our lives
We pray for every day.

You came to us long ago,
You came down from above.
Your birth as man at Bethlehem
Shows us the Father's love.

You will come again someday
To fulfill our human story.
The dead will rise up to the skies,
When you come in your great glory.

Come to us once more, O Lord,
In prayer and Sacrament.
Draw us to yourself, O Christ,
In these signs, heaven sent.

Show us now your face, O Lord,
In the poor and hungry, too.
What we do to others, Lord,
We do unto you.

O come to us, O Jesus, come,
Come to us today.
Your advent into our hearts,
We pray for every day.

193.

Advent

Today we begin Advent time,
Be open and awake.
Rise and open up your eyes,
Awaken! Sleep forsake.

Be awake to God who comes.
He comes with peace and love.
He calls us all to faith and trust.
He comes from up above.

Be awake within yourself.
Know your possibilities.
Stir these up within your soul:
Faith, love and generosity.

Be awake to others' needs.
Go beyond self-centeredness.
See the hurt and poverty,
Heal the pain and loneliness.

Advent's here. Wake up and watch.
He once came for our sake,
He comes again to fill your life.
He'll come, if you're awake.

194.

Prepare His Way

The King is coming, coming soon,
Get ready now to welcome Him.
He is our Lord and Savior King,
He comes to save, not to condemn.

The road is risky, dangerous.
Holes and hills and windy paths
Deter, delay, divert his way.
This rough road won't let him pass.

I must change my heart, my life,
Truly, my sins, I must repent.
My sin delays the coming King.
I have been so disobedient.

Pride and hatred, self-centeredness
Mountains and hills to cross,
My lack of faith, failure to love,
Alas, I feel so lost.

Jesus, Lord, come now to me,
Help me repent my sins,
Come into my heart and life,
So I may be whole again.

195.

Prepare

Jesus, help us to prepare
For when you come again.
You will come to me at death,
And at the very end.

In Advent time we do prepare
For Christmas joy and peace.
When you come into our lives.
May our love increase.

You come to us everyday
In service, love and prayer.
You touch our inner soul and heart
You are always there.

Help us to be ready, Lord,
To greet you when you come.
Give us faith, give us hope,
All fears to overcome.

Jesus, Lord, you are here,
Make me now aware
You want me to be closer, Lord,
Help me to prepare.

CHRISTMAS

197.

Bethlehem Babe

O eternal gift of love,
Gift of infinite worth,
In your birth at Bethlehem,
You bring joy to all the earth.

Joy at your becoming one
With our humanity,
We share now your very life,
We share divinity.

O child who made his mother,
Through you the world was made.
You became our brother
When we, in sin, had strayed.

Be born again, Bethlehem Babe,
Be with us, never part.
Be born with peace and love and joy,
Be born into our hearts.

198.

Bethlehem Star

Bethlehem Star, shining so bright,
Pointing the way through darkest night,
A sign of hope, even today,
For travelers of faith, now on our way.

The pathway of faith is hard and long,
Doubts and temptations can be so strong.
The Magi brought the best that they could,
They never gave up, though some thought they would.

You are our light, Christ ever new,
Your love and your Gospel draw us to you.
You are the Way, the Truth, and the Light,
Jesus, O Lord, shine ever bright.

May we mirror your light in our land,
Giving support wherever we can,
Shining like stars to help guide the way,
By service and love given each day.

Lead us, O Lord, to your "House of Bread",
The manger of life, so we may be fed
With heavenly food, in ritual,
Fed with the food of life spiritual.

Bethlehem Star, shine on us now,
With wisdom and faith, our lives endow.
Jesus, we bring you the gift of our hearts,
Be with us, Lord, never to part.

199.

Child Of Bethlehem

Jesus, Child of Bethlehem,
Come within our hearts again.
Restore our childlike spirit, Lord,
And touch the child within.

Innocent babe, perfect, pure,
Inspire true penitence,
Mercy and forgiveness bring,
Restore our innocence.

Show us how much we are loved,
Give peace, all fear destroy,
Touch the child within us, Lord,
Fill us with childlike joy.

Knowing that your love for us
Is perfect, sent from above,
Help us share with everyone,
Your gifts of joy, of love.

Jesus, Child of Bethlehem,
Come within our hearts again.
Restore our childlike spirit, Lord,
And touch the child within.

200.

Christmas Blessings

The sky is gray and trees are bare;
A hint of snow is in the air.
The fire in the hearth now burns low,
There's a scent of pine and mistletoe.

As Christmas time is almost here,
And the year's end also near,
Alone, I ponder in my heart
All the blessings you impart.

I thank thee, Lord, for my life,
So full of blessings, free of strife,
For health and peace, I thank thee,
I thank thee, Lord, for family.

For children's laughter and their smiles,
Their free spirits hearts beguile.
Hugs and kisses they freely give,
Their liveliness helps me live.

For work, and leisure time to kill,
For my abilities and skill,
For your caring without end,
For peace and joy, for my friends -

I thank thee, Lord, for them all,
All my blessings, great and small.
I love you for your loving care.
"Thank You" is my Christmas prayer.

201.

Christmas Light

A star shines bright on a winter's night.
It is a sign of hope.
No matter how dark the world may be,
We know that we will cope.

Life and love will triumph here,
No matter what may come.
The eternal God has entered time;
He has the victory won.

W are not alone, you see,
In our human frailty.
The Word made Flesh is now our guest;
He shares our humanity.

The angels sang to shepherd boys,
"Peace on earth" from up above.
So live today with peace and joy.
Christ is born because of love.

202.

Come, Little Prince

Come Little Prince, O prince of Peace.
Into our lives and hearts,
Come with your peace, come with your joy,
Come to us, ne'er to part.

You bring hope to the fearful
And joy to all forlorn.
John leapt in Elizabeth's womb
Joy-filled before being born.

Your presence among us is power,
Your gracious pardon brings peace,
Born into our hearts with joy,
Your love for us will not cease.

Come Prince of Peace, O Little Prince,
Be born in this world anew,
Help us to see you, Help us to serve you
In all that we say and do.

203.

Emmanuel

Jesus is the Word of God,
God's teaching from above.
Listen to his special Word,
His Word is endless love.

Jesus is the Lamb of God.
For us he gave not wealth,
He loves us all so perfectly,
He sacrificed himself.

Jesus is the Son of God,
A baby meek and mild
One of us, he came for this:
Each is God's own child.

God is with us in the Lord.
Have faith, the Good News tell:
In him earth and heav'n meet,
God with us, Emmanuel.

204.

Gift of the Magi

Jesus, Lord, the nations come
To worship You in awe.
Son of Mary, Son of God
On bended knee we fall.

You are God, yet born a babe
Lying in Bethlehem's cave.
Amidst the darkest gloom of night
You have come to save.

King of Kings and Lord of Lords
The Magi bring You gifts,
Gold, frankincense and myrrh,
Star-led through the mist.

What will I bring as my gift,
To you, O Savior King?
My faith, my prayer, my love, my life,
These are the gifts I bring.

Bless our lives with hope and peace,
Then our hearts will sing.
Let mercy, peace, and also joy,
Be the gifts You bring.

205.

Good News

"Good News, Good News!" the angel said.
The Savior lies in Bethlehem's bed.
A manger where oxen usually are fed
Holds food for the world, our spiritual bread.

The Good News is this: "God loves us so."
He sent his Son, even though
His Son would die, before heaven's foe,
So that we salvation would know.

The Good News proclaim, "Jesus is born!"
The'ternal Word in flesh is adorned,
He came as a babe to a world so forlorn,
That our lives not be eternally mourned.

The Good News share: "Jesus is here!"
Shout it out loud, let everyone hear,
As branches to vine, He is so near,
United to us destroying all fear.

So live in peace; we have wept enough,
Let hope fill your life from heaven above,
Let mercy fall gently on earth like a dove.
Christ is now born, incarnate love.

206.

Hidden Jesus

Sometimes the greatest things
Come disguised, without fanfare.
You can miss them easily.
You have to watch, and deeply care.

Like long ago on a quiet night
In a humble shepherd's cave,
An event occurred which no one knew
The world from death would save.

Jesus, Savior of the World,
Born in poverty,
King of Kings and Lord of Lords,
Hidden in obscurity.

There were no royal trappings there,
Your courtiers were sheep.
Your regal bed was made of straw,
The goats sang you to sleep.

You appeared in infant's clothes,
The mystery we assess:
Son of God, yet human, too,
You are the Word made Flesh.

Mary holds you in her arms,
Joseph is beguiled.
Though you are the Son of God,
You look just like any child.

Don't let us miss your presence now
In Word and in the poor.
You are here in Eucharist,
With us evermore.

You come to us in others, too,
You come in great disguise.
Your presence, give to us, O Lord,
Faith to recognize.

Hidden Jesus, in disguise,
Help us see you more.
We bring to you our trust and love,
We prostrate and adore.

207.

Holy Family

God most loving and divine,
You are gracious and most kind.
In your Son's Nativity,
You make us your own family.

In the time before he's grown
We learn about his holy home.
O God, our Father, help us see,
Help us at home to be holy.

Loving unconditionally,
Forgiving the other's frailty,
Help us your love to reflect,
In showing honor and respect.

Help us to pray to you above,
Help us to give and share our love.
Never let your mercy cease,
Fill our home with joy and peace.

208.

Make Room In Your Heart

Jesus came so long ago
A baby Mary bore,
They traveled far to Bethlehem,
Cold and tired and poor.

There was no room for them there
In the inn for travelers.
They found a cave in which to rest.
A barn for animals.

There Mary had her baby,
A baby, meek and mild.
Son of God and son of man,
He came, a little child.

This child would grow to become
The Savior of us all.
He would give his life for us,
Reversing Adam's fall.

Let him come into your heart,
Prepare a place for him.
Have faith and love for this child,
Give him a place within.

209.

Shelter Him

Jesus, Lord, are you the one
Who came to rule the earth
Have you come in God's place
To bring peace and love to birth?

When you walked this earth of ours
You touched the poor and lame,
You brought sight, and health, and life,
You call us to do the same.

Your Kingdom is not yet complete.
We must each now do our part,
Reaching out with help and love,
Giving from the heart.

When you came so long ago,
There was no room for you
In the place where travelers lodged.
A simple cave made do.

But now, dear Lord, when you come,
Find shelter in our souls.
Touch our lives with your grace,
Come and make us whole.

EASTER

210.

Alleluia

"Alleluia", my heart sings,
You are risen, glorified.
As a seed to flow'r transformed,
You live anew, though crucified.

But the best part, Jesus, Lord,
Through all our worldly strife,
You walk with us and give us hope,
You share with us your life.

Life forever, joined to you,
Triumphant, risen Lord,
You are bound to us on earth,
You, whom we adore.

We believe that with your grace,
In life's troubles, we will cope.
Death has no pow'r. We fear not.
Risen Jesus, you're our hope.

"Alleluia" is our song.
Because of love, death is destroyed/
"Alleluia", Jesus, Lord!
You share with us peace and joy.

211.

De Profundis

Because you live, we live too,
O Jesus, risen Lord.
You have triumphed o'er the grave,
Before You, we adore.

From the depths of pain and hurt,
We lift our mournful cry,
We bring our loss, we bring our dead.
Hear our grieving sigh.

Replace our pain with hope and joy,
Touch our aching hearts.
Help us understand, O Lord,
Death is but a start.

Because you love us so, O Lord,
Death is not the end.
Because you died upon the cross,
With you, we ascend.

We ascend with you, O Lord,
In death, you intervene.
We are given glory, Lord,
No mortal eye has seen.

Because you live, we live too,
O Jesus, risen Lord.
You have triumphed o'er the grave.
Before you, we adore.

212.

Death's Power Destroyed

Risen Jesus, victorious Lord,
You destroyed death's pow'r.
So that we should not be afraid
Of death at our last hour

Because you live, we shall live
In body and in soul.
Death defeated, we shall rise
Alive, glorified, whole.

Free us from all fear, O Lord,
Let us all be free
From fear of losing out in life,
For death will come to me.

But death is not the end of things
We will someday rise
In body and in soul alive,
And fly above the sky.

Help us all now live aright,
Living to the full,
In justice, love and peace, O Lord,
Death's pow'r you annul.

213.

Jesus Alive

The dirge and the wailing, the sadness and grief,
Comes like the night, comes like a thief,
Comes with dark malice, comes from beneath.

Where is hope buried? Where is love's grave?
Where is my Savior who came for to save,
Who came to this earth, who came for to save?

My Jesus, my life, my hope and my heart,
What have they done? Why do you part?
Where are you going? From us you depart.

But look in the tomb. The body's not there.
Someone has taken my Savior somewhere.
The tomb is now empty, empty and bare.

Faith has its reason; reason needs faith.
Our Savior has risen! Follow with haste.
The Savior has risen, his truth you must taste.

Jesus in glory, Jesus alive!
Jesus, our Savior, for us you have died.
For our life eternal, you cast death aside.

Be with us, Jesus, dry every tear.
Love is victorious! Love destroys fear!
Jesus, be with us; be always near.

214.

Jesus Lives

Jesus, you have triumphed, Lord!
The chains of death, you broke.
You deliver us from death,
You have taken off our yoke.

You are our deliverer,
Our champion, our King.
Because you live, we now live,
Your praises, Lord, we sing.

"Alleluia" is our song,
Free us from sin and strife.
You forever are our King,
You change death to life.

Unless the seed should die, you said,
It shall not ever live.
Through death and resurrection, Lord,
Your life to us you give.

We must die to selfishness.
In generous love, sin dies.
Entering death with you, O Lord,
In you O Lord, we rise.

We rise in life eternal, Lord,
Joy replaces Friday's gloom,
That which gives us peace and hope,
Is your empty tomb.

215.

Jesus Victorious

Alleluia, the Victory won,
He is risen, Christ the Son,
For all mankind, crucified,
On Calvary's cross, he has died.
But the grave could not him hold,
The tomb is empty, barren, cold.

Why do you mourn, why do you cry?
In Jesus' death, death did die.
He is victorious o'er the grave,
Jesus has won; we are saved.
Rejoice O children, lift up your head.
Jesus lives, no longer dead.

Evil, hatred, seek to destroy,
But we live in hope and joy.
Don't give up; don't give in,
Christ in glory destroys all sin.
Jesus, our end, our origin,
Have confidence! Have hope in Him,

Choose life, not death, choose victory,
Believe that which cannot be seen.
Jesus is here, victorious,
The victory he shares with us.
Know, when evil your soul demands,
The Shepherd holds you in his hands.

216.

Easter Jesus

Easter Jesus, Son of God,
Calvary's road you have trod,
Whipped and stripped and crucified,
For our salvation, you have died,
Opening heaven's portals wide.

You are risen, glorified,
Changed, transformed, and you abide
As one with all in faith you find
Joined as branches to the vine,
As body to its head aligned.

Unlike Lazarus, you arose
Glorified. The Father chose
That you should be like a seed
Planted, buried, guaranteed
To rise, transformed, totally.

You call us, Jesus, to be one
In your church and to become
Your witnesses to reveal
Your love and power that we feel
To our world, you died to heal.

Easter Jesus, help us believe.
Take away our doubts. Relieve
Our fears. Our faith and hope renew.
May our hearts be ever true
In loving and in serving you.

MARY

217.

Assumption Prayer

Mary, Mother, Queen revered,
To the Father, so endeared,
You were taken bodily
Into heaven, joyfully,
To be with God eternally.

Sinless woman, you were given,
This share in Jesus' glory risen,
All through life you said "yes",
To serve God's will, your only quest,
Your love for him is measureless.

You are a sign to us on earth,
A promised pledge of heaven's birth,
To us, if faithfully we live
Life loving, faithful, positive,
Eternal life God will give.

Body and soul we will be
With Jesus and you eternally.
Glorified. O Mary, Queen illustrious,
Mother of Christ, victorious,
Please, dear Mary, pray for us.

218.

Blessed Virgin

Jesus Lord, how great your plan:
To save you came to earth.
Mary was your instrument,
A virgin, whose virgin birth
Brings God to those who thirst.

Blessed Virgin, sinless too,
In her virginity,
She expresses emptiness,
To be filled with Divinity,
Sign of our own destiny.

Jesus, Lord for you we thirst,
Come, with us abide,
Fill us with your Spirit, Lord,
Our hearts, now occupy,
Be with us, walk beside.

Like Mary, we now wait for you,
To be our divine guest,
We wait with love and eagerness,
We are truly blessed,
With Mary, we say "Yes"!

219.

Guadalupe Virgin

Guadalupe Virgin,
Advent's peasant Queen,
Point the way to faith today,
To hidden Christ, unseen.

He was born in poverty,
You are also poor.
He calls us all to value more
Than riches, heaven's store.

He was hidden in your womb,
In your time of patient faith,
Waiting, longing, filled with love.
In love, our hopes are based.

Jesus, come into our hearts
As into Mary's womb.
You came with life and love and joy.
Jesus, please come soon.

Help us to reform our lives.
May your will be done.
Create in us true harmony,
Jesus, Lord, please come.

Guadalupe Virgin,
Advent's peasant Queen,
Point the way to love today,
To hidden Christ, unseen.

220.

Immaculate Mary

Hail Mary, Mother of God,
Mother of Jesus, our Lord,
Filled with God's grace and his love,
On us that grace is outpoured.

Mary, dear Mother of Jesus,
Sinless from your earthly start,
We are your sinful children,
We appeal to your motherly heart.

Pray for us now, dear Mother,
Blest like no other one.
Your example, teach us to follow,
Help us to follow your son.

You always said "yes" to the Father,
Grace always came from above.
You are our model believer.
Teach us to trust and to love.

Immaculate Mary, we love you,
Conceived without primal sin,
God always dwelling within you,
Our Model, our Mother, our Friend.

221.

Mary

O Mary, Mother of the Lord,
Your praises now we sing.
You are truly Mother of God,
To you our love we bring.

Jesus is the true Son of God,
Divine Lord and brother,
Through him everything came to be,
And you are his dear Mother.

On Calvary he gave to us
A gift to help us through
This vale of tears and challenges.
You are our Mother, too.

We are your children, every one,
Your love is glorious.
In all our trials and suffering,
You intercede for us.

You are the Mother of the Church,
In faith and love you give
The way that we should emulate,
You show us how to live.

You care about each one of us
Your love is ever true,
Be near us always, dear Mother,
O Mary, we love you.

222.

Visitation

Mary, Queen, and Mother mine,
Greatest Mother of all time,
You said "yes" to God's request,
And Jesus came to be our guest.

Humble maiden, lowly one,
You told God, "Your will be done,"
Your loving sprit well He knew,
Greatly He exalted you.

Knowing of your cousin's need,
To her side you did proceed.
At your greeting, though asleep,
In her womb, the child did leap.

Mary, you brought Christ to John.
Your gift we depend upon.
In our need, bring Christ to us,
Help us, Mother glorious.

You are Mother of the Church,
You reign o'er the universe.
You brought Christ the world into,
Help us bring your Son there too.

GENERAL

223.

A Blessing for Mom

We thank you, Lord, for our Moms,
What precious gifts they are
To us, their children, in your plan,
Like brilliant, sparkling stars.

Their light shines brightly in our lives,
Life's lessons they have taught,
What's right and wrong, and good and bad,
How life's battles should be fought.

Motherhood means their gift of life
But gift of Spirit too,
They lead the way to holiness,
To happiness, to You.

Jesus, Lord, bless them today
With joy, and love, and peace,
Help them to know how much they're loved,
May your blessing never cease.

224.

A Prayer For Mother

Thank you, O God, for our mother,
A force in Life like none other.
She gives of self, not counting cost,
She loves and prays lest we be lost.

Thank you, Lord, for her concern
That we grow and that we learn
To fulfill your plan for us,
Becoming merciful and just.

Bless her, Lord, with peace and joy.
All her worries, please destroy.
Bless her home, and bless her heart,
Your gift of happiness impart.

Bless her family with peace.
All divisions, let them cease.
Fill her heart with a mother's pride
With her children at her side.

May her pride ever grow,
As time goes by, let her know
In her role, she did excel,
As a mother, she did well.

225.

A Prayer For Our Graduates

Bless, O Lord, our graduates,
These youths so full of life.
Enrich their faith, keep them safe,
Give strength to them in strife.

Help them to know we love them so,
How wonderful they are.
If they believe in themselves,
They'll live fully and go far.

Help them trust their families,
Their parents are so proud.
They live and give and sacrifice,
Their children to endow.

Help them love you, Jesus Lord.
Steer them through life's storms.
Be the rudder of their ship,
Keep them from all harm.

226.

Cedars

A cedar wall, wildly dense
Shades of blackened green
Arrogant, against the field
Unbroken, savage, mean.

But not so callous as not to save
Turkeys nesting high
In branches rough and menacing
A haven, if you fly.

Some folks are cedar built,
Rough and prickly red
Hardened by life's onslaught
Pain and violence fed.

Surviving, the important goal,
Living for the day,
Against the odds of choice and chance,
"I'm here, and here I'll stay."

Defiant always, nonetheless,
When occasions rise,
Shelter they might offer you
If you also try.

227.

Desert Dawn

As night gives way to tinsled dawn
And clouds in priestly garb adore
Like red-robed martyrs queued to the horizon
I greet Thee and bow down

As Thou break open heaven's doors
Closed and latched in dark and fear
Break open other doors
Barricaded hopelessly against the light

As celestial fingers inspect
The purple-black billows of your night watchmen
Awarding them red-golden ribbons for their valor
Touch my heart with morning glory

Today give me mind to search
Eyes to see and heart to love
And though clouds heavy with grayness roll back in mid-morning
Remind me of the dawn—and your abiding love

228.

God With Skin On

O Jesus, Lord, our risen King,
I want to see you, touch your skin,
To know you're here, to know you're real,
With you to triumph and to win.

I know you're here, with us now,
You teach us with your word.
Your word is life, your word is truth,
Refuting the absurd.

You're here in the Bread and Wine,
Sacraments of love,
You touch through them our minds and hearts,
You come down from above.

We touch now your glorious being,
In the fellowship we share,
In caring, service and sharing, Lord,
To each other, You, we bear.

You are not a ghostly soul;
Over death you have won.
Risen Word of God, enfleshed,
You are God, with skin on.

229.

Guatemalan Palette

Jesus comes in bright colors.
I saw him yesterday in blue and red,
Wrapped round a suckling child
Tied to mother as he fed.

He was there in chocolate brown
Furrowed face, orbed with blackened lights,
Supporting a heavy load
Of bundled firewood, all wrapped tight.

I saw him too, in sparkling white
Laughing teeth of a five year old,
Stunted, without much food,
Playing with a giant. He was bold!

Jesus came with rainbow hue,
Inspiring smiles of adoration
On those who recognized her,*
And knew the hope of liberation.

Jesus at Mass in Host of white,
Like a prism splitting light,
Your paint splatters everywhere,
Rainbow Jesus, give me sight.

Colorful Jesus, you are here
In evergreen hope midst purple pain,
In self-sacrificing red you are clothed,
With indelible hue, my life come stain.

*On the occasion of the talk by Nobel Prize winner, Rigoberta Menchu to Guatemalan
refugees in January, 1993, in Chimaltenango, Guatemala.

230.

Mother

You are the source of who I am,
Who I am is also new.
I am from God, the world, myself,
But also I come from you.

Without you, I would not be,
You gave me life, you gave me birth.
You birthed my body, spirit too.
You birthed in me my own self-worth.

Birthing takes place in teaching trust,
In holding close and feeding too.
In body and in spirit feed,
With words of love, you birth anew.

Birthing comes in many ways,
In vanquishing my foes.
In teaching, touching, listening too,
You watch your children grow.

How many times you have cried
Out loud. It also was inward,
When you felt or saw the pain,
Or hurt or trial your child endured.

You are one with your offspring.
You feel our joys and sorrows too.
You cannot help but share our pain,
Yet you choose all that you do.

Strong and fierce and tender too,
You cry, you laugh, your share your life,
You nurture, give and you protect,
You know well, self-sacrifice.

With God you give us life and love,
You give to us like no other.
For God and child you sacrifice.
I speak with love the words, "My Mother".

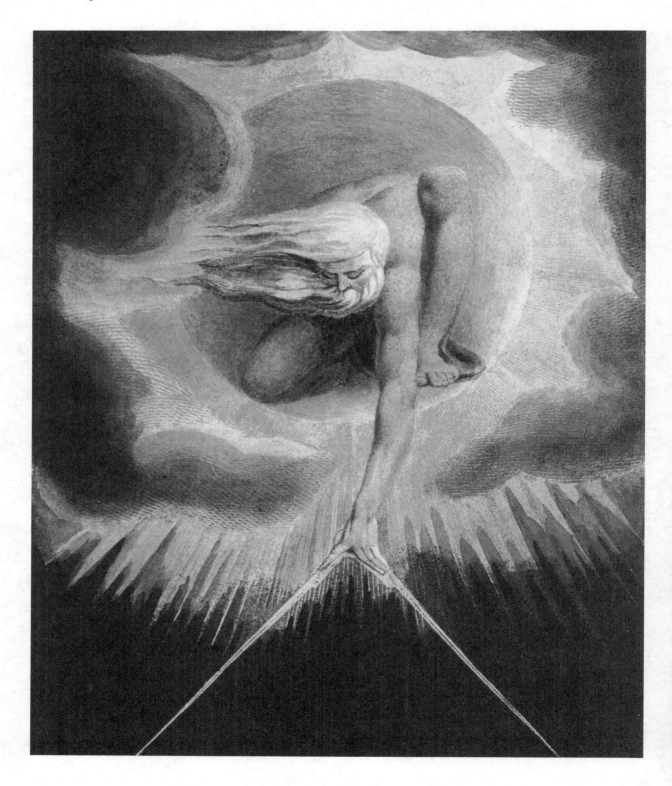

231.

Planting

It's a peculiar thing,
The business of planting.
You take living seeds,
Dormant though they be,
And bury them.
Like anything you bury,
They die.

At least their life is changed
And becomes something new,
Still the same seeds, but something new.
They die to themselves,
Like acorns rooting,
Like cocoons morphing,
Like us surrendering, loving,
dying.

Anyway, what am I willing to bury in the ground?
What am I planting?
For what would I give up my life?
Would I give up my life for you?
Someone did, you know.

232.

Prayer for a Baptism

Thank you, Lord, for all your gifts
We have such gratitude,
For this child, your special gift
In her, your love's renewed.

She is so precious in your sight,
So sweet and innocent,
A miracle here, before our eyes,
Your love, magnificent!

Today through living waters here,
Your Spirit enters her.
She is a temple where you dwell,
Your life with her you share.

Child of God, she has become,
Loved from all eternity,
Born again, to be one with you;
Heaven is her destiny.

Bless this child throughout her life,
Fill her heart with praise.
Grant her faith and happiness,
Give love to her always.

233.

Prayer For Our Youth

Jesus, Lord, protect our youth,
Keep them close to you.
The world invites with its allure,
False values to pursue.

Temptation looms so subtley,
In the world in which they live,
To choose the false, the bad, the wrong,
To take, and not to give.

Guard them, Lord, help them to live
In purity of heart.
Fill them with faith, with hope and love,
Virtues and grace impart.

Consecrate them to yourself,
Let them be leaven, salt,
To change the world for love of you,
In you, let them exalt.

Help them to know how You love them,
Help them see the truth,
Bless them with wisdom and your grace,
Lord, protect our youth.

234.

Prayer For Priests

Jesus Lord, our great High Priest
Be with us today.
Bless our priests with holiness
Keep them on your way.

Give them wisdom, give them grace
To heal, to give, to serve
All those you have given them,
To love, without reserve.

Help them to be men of prayer,
With you first in their lives,
Grant compassion, humility,
Let joy in them arise.

With joy and great devotion,
Help them celebrate
The sacred mysteries you give,
Our souls to consecrate.

Forgive their sins, help them grow
In holiness of life
To bring to us your blessing, Lord,
And peace in midst of strife.

Send us more vocations, Lord,
Young men who want to serve
You and all your people, Lord,
Our faith we ask, preserve.

235.

Prayer of Parents

Jesus, help me parent
My child with faith and love.
Send to me your wisdom
Your help from up above.

Give me the words that I need
To teach important truth,
So they'll know how to live well
Even from their youth.

Help me model faith for them
So that faith will grow.
While living in this sinful world,
You, Jesus they will know.

Help me show what true love is.
They need more than words.
They need to feel, and see love
Expressed in life, outwards.

Jesus, come, be here with me
Teach me how to parent
My children whom I dearly love.
They're truly heaven-sent.

236.

The Church, God's Gift

Jesus Lord, we today rejoice
In your gift of love
You richly give us all our lives
Your blessing from above.

Thank you for this beautiful church
Gleaming like the stars
You are here, O loving Lord,
Thank you for Cure of Ars.

Here we celebrate your presence, Lord,
Here you come to us,
As we observe the mysteries
We grow in love and trust.

O Jesus, you were crucified,
But you are arisen,
You gave all, and you are here,
You impart wisdom.

Wisdom to choose what brings life
To live life to the fullest,
To love you Lord, with all our hearts
To love you, and to trust.

We trust you, O most gracious Lord,
You love in all you do,
And you command that we must
Love our neighbor, too.

237.

We are Cure'

We are Cure' of Ars, O Lord,
Your people who believe.
For fifty years we've been your church;
Your blessings we've received.

For fifty years we've served you, Lord,
We've prayed and worked and shared
The faith and truth you gave us, Lord,
Because we really cared.

We cared enough to sow and plant
The seeds of love and joy.
The seeds of hope and endless life,
So death you would destroy.

We honor you, O Lord, our God,
On this our jubilee,
Now we pray that you bless us, Lord
Through St. John Vianney.

Bless our families, and bless our world,
We need your graces, Lord,
Bring us your peace, and then someday
Give us your great reward.

LIST OF IMAGES

Cover
Face of Christ–Shroud Of Turin, Artistic Rendering

Adoration and Praise
Bridge to Eternal Life–Mural, Church of the Nativity, Bethlehem, Israel
Holy Trinity–Painting, Church of the Holy Sepulchre, Jerusalem, Israel
Transfigured–Fra Angelico, Transfiguration, Circa 1437-1446
With Eyes Fixed On Jesus–Carl Bloch, The Sermon On The Mount, 1876

Discipleship
At the Well–Mural, Church of Jacob's Well, Nablus, Israel
Humble Jesus–Painting of Jesus Washing Peter's Feet by Ford Madox Brown
No Other Hands- Mosaic, Jerusalem, Israel
World On Fire–Stained Glass Window, Church of the Nativity, Bethlehem, Israel

Faith, Hope, Love
Cana Prayer–Painting, The Wedding Church at Cana, Cana, Israel
I Trust You Lord–Mural, Stella Maris Monastery on Mt. Carmel, Nazareth, Israel
Shepherd of My Soul–Painting of The Good Shepherd by Bernhard Plockhorst

Sin and Forgiveness
Cleansing the Temple–Bernardino Mei: Christ Cleansing the Temple
Divine Mercy–Painting, Notre Dame of Jerusalem Center, Jerusalem, Israel
Sweet Temptation–Christ in the Wilderness–Ivan Kramskoy

The Cross
Friday's Love–Fra Angelico, The Crucified Christ, Circa 1437-1446
Woman Behold your Son–Lucas Cranach d. Ä.–The Lamentation of Christ, 1503
And Jesus Wept–Relief, Home of Caiaphas, Jerusalem, Israel
Triumphant Cross–Benjamin West, The Ascension, 1800
Your Cross–Mural, Church of the Nativity, Bethlehem, Israel

Eucharist
Emmaus Lord–Zünd Gang nach Emmaus, Road To Emmaus, 1877
Prepare His Way–Mural, Stella Maris Monastery on Mt. Carmel, Nazareth, Israel
The Body and Blood of Christ–Christ with the Eucharist, Vicente Juan Masip, 16th century.

Christmas
Bethlehem Star–Silver & Marble Marker, Photograph by Michael McGlinn, Church of the Nativity, Bethlehem, Israel
Christmas Light–Painting, Church of the Nativity, Bethlehem, Israel
Gift of the Magi–Adoration of the Magi by Bartolomé Esteban Murillo
Hidden Jesus–Mural, Stella Maris Monastery on Mt. Carmel, Nazareth, Israel

Easter
Jesus Alive–Mural, Monastery of Temptation, Jericho, Israel

Mary
Guadalupe Virgin–A depiction of Virgin of Guadalupe, from 1779, Mexico
Immaculate Mary–Fra Angelico, Annunciation, 1437-46

General
Desert Dawn–Gustave Doré, Paradise Canto, 1892
Planting–William Blake, Europe A Prophecy, 1794

CPSIA information can be obtained
at www.ICGtesting.com
Printed in the USA
FSOW03n0004160316
18072FS